The Rise of a New Breed

APMI Publications
a division of Kingdom Dimension Books
P.O. Box 17,
55051 Barga (LU),
Tuscany, Italy

EMMANUEL SARFO
ACHEAMPONG

The Rise of a New Breed

"Unstained by the culture and tradition of men"

HUNGRY BOOK SERIES ONE

BOOK TITLE:
The Rise of a New Breed

WRITTEN BY EMMANUEL SARFO ACHEAMPONG
ISBN: 978-1-918102-05-5
eBook ISBN: 978-1-918102-06-2

Copyright 2025 Emmanuel Sarfo Acheampong

All rights reserved under International Copyright Law. Contents and/or cover may not be reproduced in whole or in part in any form without the express written consent of the Publisher.

Published by APMI Publications
A Division of Kingdom Dimension Books
P.O. Box 17,
55051 Barga (LU),
Italy

Email: publications@alanpatemanworldmissions.com
www.AlanPatemanWorldMissions.com

Acknowledgements:
Cover Design Copyright APMI
Senior Editor/Publisher: Dr. Alan Pateman
Editing/Proofreading/Research: Dr. Jennifer Pateman
Computer Administration/Office Manager: Dr. Dorothea Struhlik
Cover Image Credit: www.PosterMyWall.com

*Where scriptures appear with special emphasis (**in bold,** italic or underlined) we have edited them ourselves in order to bring focused attention within the context of this subject being taught.*

Dedication

To the person who is genuinely and
desperately hungry for God.
Matthew 5:6

Table of Contents

Foreword

The book you hold is quite possibly the most important confrontation with truth you will encounter in your lifetime. A book that serves as both a companion and a guide can encourage readers to pause, reflect, and consider different viewpoints. This volume, which you now hold in your hands, is just such a treasure: it is a testament to the enduring power of a new breed that cries out for more of God Himself, and the written Word to shape the way we see God and ourselves.

The dynamic teachings and encouragement of the author **Emmanuel Sarfo Acheampong** draws the hearts of believers and non-Christians into a deeper hunger, searching for an intimacy to pursue the only Saviour and Lord for life—Jesus Christ.

As the author penned these opening thoughts, I am reminded that every book is an invitation—a threshold across which we step, leaving behind the familiar and venturing into landscapes crafted by imagination, experience, and wisdom. The pages that follow are not merely repositories of information or entertainment, but the result of passion, curiosity, and a deep commitment to truth.

The author whose work unfolds here has poured heart and mind into every chapter. Drawing from years of study, training, observation, and lived experience, they have woven together themes that resonate across time and place. The subjects explored are not only relevant but urgent, asking us to think more critically and empathetically about the issues of our salvation. Whether you are seeking fresh insight, timeless wisdom, or want to know Jesus Christ—not in a religious way but with personal intimacy—you will find it here.

The author admonishes his fellow younger generations to embrace the opportunity for the mentorship of the fathers which are the core values and foundations for every successful generation throughout history. Fathers were expected to build relationships with their children to encourage obedience and receive blessings instead of curses. *"And he will turn the hearts of the fathers to the children, And the hearts of the children to their fathers, Lest I come and strike the earth with a curse" (Malach 4:6 NKJV).*

Notwithstanding, the book emphasised the importance of both the physical and spiritual fathers. Through the wisdom and guidance of fathers, many generations have achieved their intended purpose in the Bible.

A book is never the product of a single mind. Behind these words stand friends and mentors, critics and supporters—who have offered encouragement, challenge, and inspiration. In reading, we become a part of this insight: not passive recipients, but active participants in a conversation that stretches far beyond these pages.

We have much to learn from this young man—Emmanuel Sarfo Acheampong who made it work. Read, ***The Rise of a New Breed.*** Consume it. Digest it. Let it become part of your spiritual mettle.

It is my sincere hope that, as you read, you will find yourself pausing to question, to imagine, to remember and seeking God. May this book serve as a lantern, casting light into corners both familiar and strange, and may it stay with you long after the final page is turned.

Apostle Dr. Benjamin Ayim Asare,
Followers of Christ International Church, Novara-Italy
author of *The Anointing is the Assignment,* and
Discover Your Ministry in the Local Church

Preface

The Rise of a New Breed is a compendium of reflections directed to a begetting generation in the Body of Christ, dissatisfied with the current spiritual condition, notwithstanding the enormous display of gifts, material blessings, accomplished dreams, notable self-recognition, fame or all sorts of influence and achievements we may have attained in the current church and in society.

This breed cries out for more of God Himself. It is a true hunger for God in their dying world. I personally address a generation who has the sincere desire for the King to be enthroned and worshiped in their hearts and environment, causing their inner being to tremble at His Word as they submit themselves and surrender totally and completely as instruments of Righteousness unto God without any reservation.

After carefully observing the Church today, it is almost very clear that on one hand, self-ambition and self-fulfilment are the ultimate trophies and goals for becoming a Christian, therefore men are praised for their gifts and talents instead of the Giver of talents. On the other hand, men are told to believe that they are saved just because they once upon a time were told to repeat a prayer after the preacher.

As years pass by, such individuals learn the Christian religious language and its forms but have never been really transformed in their heart by the Holy Spirit who administers eternal life to the sinner. These philosophies are ripping the Body of Christ of its true identity and glory bestowed upon it by her Groom.

We are supplanting the Kingdom life-giving message of our Lord and His apostles, which was laid as the foundation, and what the early church laboured for, with the message of self and man centeredness, which arms the devil to blind us of the power of the Holy Spirit. Self, the flesh and temporal gain is the message of today.

The cross, the sacrificial life of Jesus and that of the believer has been done away, as well as total surrender to the Holy Spirit and dying to one's own desire and passion for the cause of the Kingdom of God. Totally laying everything at the feet of the cross is old-fashioned and tarrying before God is a burdensome experience to talk about.

The message of Babylon that proclaims greatness—not holiness—is cheered, embraced and highly applauded. Crowns are simply offered without a cross. It is the influence of the spirit of Jezebel, which seduces the messenger and his message, so that the people of God may commit idolatry and play harlotry.

The Church is influenced by the world, while the world still rejects the Builder of the Church and His Holy Words! Notwithstanding the tremendous advancements in finance, technology and healthcare in our modern society, there is a generation that seems to be—almost, if not totally—alienated from the knowledge of God.

It is a culture that hates God and all that pertains to Him or is attributed to Him—especially His Church. The name of God is blasphemed openly in public, revealing the deep disdain society holds toward Him. We live in a highly dissatisfied and confused world—a society that offers many solutions, yet cannot solve the core issue of the human heart.

In all this, there is a generation that is gradually getting into deeper grounds with the devil, while rejecting God. It embraces every philosophy that centres on the concept of self-fulfilment. Man is the idol in our world today and he is prioritised above everything. A message that appeases even the believer in Christ.

This has progressively broken the firm structures of society, leaving a generation totally empty and in a futile search of their true identity. A generation hungry for something it cannot explain.

Many young people in the West today have plunged into various philosophical and spiritual movements such as Buddhism, Hinduism, Spiritualist Associations, the New Age, and spiritual meditation clubs—many of which originate from Eastern occultic practices. These are rapidly flourishing in Western societies that have forgotten their Judeo-Christian foundations.

Such practices are demonic portals that draws innocent people—especially my generation—into an unknown and dangerous world. It's a restlessness in the souls of men. An inner void many seek to fill. A hunger for the supernatural, yet it is only through the right door that one can access the true and living God—His love, peace and joy—that is found in the person of Jesus Christ.

He is the only approved and tested way, the truth and the life. He is willing to make Himself known to all who will call on His name and are willing to draw closer to Him. Only in Him can we find our true self and purpose.

I sincerely desire through this little book to present man's ultimate goal of life and the very One he eagerly yearns for, that is the Lord Jesus. He is the only solution for mankind, provided by God, in every generation and in every season.

Furthermore, this is written to exalt the youth of this generation—like myself—whose hearts are dying for a deeper intimacy with the true God, and who long to go beyond the superficial rituals and culture of mere Christianity *(religion)*, pressing on until we enter the fullness of the reality that is available to all who seek Him and His Kingdom purposes.

That we may be carriers of God—living to please Him—and become channels and useful instruments in our season, glowing in His glory and imparting to the coming generation as well. He is the only reason we live, and He is the totality of all that every human being needs.

Acknowledgement

I have to start by thanking a special person. God gave men gifts and talents but He gave me a wife, the best He had in heart for me after saving my soul. Federica, you literally pulled this material out of me.

A special thanks to my mom and dad for building a godly home and for the genuine faith with which they raised me and my siblings. Notwithstanding the many challenges, their unwavering faith in God has proven to be truly trustworthy.

My sincere appreciation to Franc-Nicolas, a true friend indeed. Our numerous and tireless conversations on the subject matter have helped bring about this miracle on paper.

Without the diligent and consistent prayers of the Church, this would have remained only a desire in my heart.

May God richly bless the Friday prayer group of FOCIC—every meeting brought greater clarity.

A big "God bless you" to all who kindly shared their hearts with me through personal testimonies, reflections, and thoughts concerning the very essence of this message.

Furthermore, I cannot fail to acknowledge my spiritual father, Apostle Dr. Benjamin Ayim Asare, for being a true father to me. His corrections, reproof, encouragement, and guidance have brought me this far. I also wish to thank Dr. Alan Pateman, his wife, Dr. Jennifer, and the team at APMI Publications, whose support and contribution through publishing, editing, and design have been invaluable in bringing this work to fruition.

Introduction

This manuscript is not a call to downplay the role or the works of our fathers—the older generation. Nor is it intended to promote or ridicule any cultural practice in our society, except where such practices clearly contradict the Holy Word of God. The value of every society is rooted in the culture, traditions, and belief systems of its people.

It is not intended to undermine the Christian culture either, which, to a large extent, has shaped many parts of the world—especially the West. Some of our laws and moral codes were birthed from such endeavours, and I by no means intend to mock the efforts or the outcomes produced by the Christian cultural faith in our societies, which has paved the way for greater social and economic stability today.

Christianity—with all the weaknesses we may point out—has nevertheless been a blessing to the world as a whole. I also do not believe there is anything truly new in itself—a new move that has not, in some form, already been.

Any new move of God has already been predicted by the Scriptures and men of old have walked and tasted of it. Such as a new revival or awakening. Scripture itself makes it clear that there is nothing new under the sun. I sincerely want to clarify that this is not an essay to reject or speak evil of spiritual authorities in the local churches and in the Body of Christ or even in our civil society.

VIVID EXPERIENCES & ENCOUNTERS

Neither do I advocate for a generation to rebel against their fathers in the faith, to whom we owe our upbringing in the Lord. I do not seek to create any confusion or reformation of any kind. He is indeed the God of Abraham, Isaac and Jacob, the God of individuals, families and generations.

> He will turn the hearts of the fathers to their children, and the hearts of the children to their fathers [a reconciliation produced by repentance], so that I will not come and strike the land with a curse [of complete destruction].
>
> Malachi 4:6 AMP

Abraham knew Him as the El Shaddai, the God who provides; Isaac knew Him as Rehoboth, the God who makes room; while Jacob encountered the same God in Bethel, His house and subsequently saw Him face to face and wrestled with Him in Peniel. The same God, but different vivid and life changing experiences and encounters.

He is the God of my biological parents as well as my father in the Lord, Pastor Benjamin, who, in their humble and unwavering faith, have—and still continually do—feed me daily with the Word of God and persevere in their private prayers that my soul may not remain in the dark. In them I see faith, and I experience firsthand what it is like to be a believer.

THE BRAVERY OF THE OLDER GENERATION

The bravery of the older generation and their walk with the Lord is the essential footstep on which every younger generation must tread, in order to learn from their mistakes and capitalise on the superfluity of the grace and mercy of God they encountered on their journey.

"Look to Abraham your father, and Sarah who bore you; for I called him alone, and blessed him and increased him" (Isaiah 51:2 NKJV). We are the increase of this first family—the older generation. The life of our ancestors, Abraham and Sarah, is the life we must imitate in order to remain faithful to their God, who is also our God.

The older generation has left us a legacy and a heritage that we must cherish deeply. We ought to live by that same pattern of faith—with sincerity, integrity of heart and with all perseverance and endurance. We must be possessed with such holy virtues that we may walk with God as they faithfully did in their time.

We must therefore solemnly uphold the faith—this sacred journey that our generation must partake in—in order to see the manifestation of God. Unto them we must also look for direction and counsel. Our fathers today are instruments of the Lord to help us grow into maturity.

We shouldn't be a rebellious generation against God's delegated human authority *(whether in families, churches or civil society).* That is, unless the name of the Lord and His truth is trampled on. As a younger generation, we must respect and honour our leaders and elders in church, as they watch over our souls, Scripture says.

Unlike Korah and his pals, we must serve in truth and remain faithful to the end—with our Moses, Aaron, Miriam, and leaders in the Body of Christ. They are to be honoured, no matter what! They are our overseers, and they help keep order in the Church , family, and in society—as it is in heaven. It's rather our duty to pray for them: that they may have grace to lead properly and godly.

EVERY GENERATION—MUST DILIGENTLY SEEK GOD

A prideful generation rejects submission to authority and refuses counsel. We must not uncover the nakedness of our fathers as Ham did, procuring curses on his generation. Such a one is headed directly to destruction. Pride has won his heart. Even in misunderstandings we must honour and carefully give account to them, and above all never rebuke an older man.

Having said this, it is my sincere motivation to highlight the necessity and responsibility which rests upon every generation, to diligently seek God afresh. He reveals Himself differently and uniquely in different seasons, so that every generation will remain in alignment and in synchrony with His workings and dealings in their hearts.

Both the individual and the Body of Christ—as a corporate organism—should endeavour to seek God and the things of the Kingdom afresh. Even though our Lord is the same yesterday, today, and forever, He often works in new ways. In every season and generation, He operates uniquely in order to establish the enterprise of His Kingdom on earth.

THE CRY OF MY HEART

Furthermore, His ways are not our ways and neither are His thoughts our thoughts. He dealt with Abraham, Isaac and Jacob based on the same covenant but with each in a unique way. Indeed, there is no other supreme purpose for which we were created but to fulfil the dream and will of our God on this earth. This is the cry of my heart, as I have tried to deduce in this book.

Living experiences in the Scriptures—my little personal experiences and convictions—as well as the testimonies of some older and younger believers *(including some non-believers)* have led me to a brighter and more accurate assertion regarding the theme of this book.

As I sought God—in prayer and fasting—it always became clear to me how the Spirit of God works precisely in the hearts of men in each generation in order to help them fulfil His purposes, in every given season. No man can fully know His ways; they are as eternal as His being. Therefore, no man can manipulate His purposes on earth. Hallelujah!

PRELIMINARY CONCEPTION

Seasons are not the same, they are subject to change, and therefore every person including the believer in Christ is required to adapt a new way of confronting life affairs, according to the leading of the Holy Spirit and the Word. This new way I mention, is pointed to the same old indications made available throughout the lives of the men and women in the Holy Scriptures, who knew God and walked with Him.

We are not to forget the path of these ancient men and women, who have created patterns for us today to walk in. The Lord is the same, He of course never changes and doesn't need to adapt Himself to circumstances or the times. He is omniscient and doesn't require a new method to survive.

Nevertheless, the believer is required to seek the Lord in order to walk with Him accurately, as times change. All were written as examples to us that we may learn and be faithful to the very end, as some of them were.

DON'T QUIT KNOCKING AT THE DOORS OF HEAVEN

There won't always be persecution and suffering in our walk with God. Neither are we going to bathe in abundance all the time. It is also true that we won't experience the Lord "tangibly" as we'd love to all the time either. There are seasons of preparation, seasons of gathering, times for sowing, watering, pruning and reaping, as well as scattering. Seasons of joy and weeping, as well as abundance and lack.

Joseph and David and Queen Esther are perfect examples of people who were dealt with by God throughout various seasons. Their stories in the Bible are worth studying and emulating. All is the doing of the Lord. It is unwise to let go of the Lord and quit knocking at the doors of heaven.

When men cease praying and stop waiting on the Lord, they become comfortable with Christian rituals, ceremonies, repetitious activities, which as good as they are, have the tendency to produce no life. Culture and tradition they become, sincerely observed and practised, but can block the flow of the dynamic power of the Spirit of God, the only capable agency for producing abundant life and transformation in the heart of the believer and in society.

THE BELIEVER'S INNER PENDULUM

The Scriptures make it even clearer that our God sometimes hides Himself *(Isaiah 45:15)*. He purposely does that to try the hearts of men. Paul knew exceptionally well how unstable the pendulum could be in a believer's life—in each given season.

Therefore, he gives a remarkable platform for us in Philippians 4:12–14 *(AMP)*, *"I know how to get along and live humbly (in difficult times), and also know how to enjoy abundance and live in prosperity. In any and every circumstance I have learned the secret (of facing life), whether well-fed or going hungry, whether having an abundance of being in need…"*

The book of Ecclesiastes in Chapter 3 verses 1–8 gives an elaborate account of the varieties of activities that can occur in every given time or season. This, I believe, applies as well to the dealings of the Spirit of God in every generation.

HE WILL NEVER LEAVE US ALONE

He will never leave us alone, but we as well have the mandate to seek Him and enforce His will to be done in our season and for the coming ones. This is a call to watch and pray without ceasing.

CHAPTER 1

Who are these Hungry People?

This brand of believers seeks only Jesus as their ultimate goal and their exceedingly great reward. In such vessels the Lord will live and operate in and through them, for the world to witness the power of the gospel. The Spirit of God in them will fully operate in accordance to their submitted will in conformity to the purposes of God.

Such ones have a unique desire for the person of Jesus to be exalted above anything else they desire in their hearts, and above all to see Jesus exalted in their society. It is indeed a hunger in the spirit of this generation to see the Church of God go beyond her programmes.

These people desire to see the Spirit of God taking over completely our fellowship to the point where men can no longer minister because the Glory of the Lord will fill the temple. In this atmosphere He is at liberty to do whatever He wills, since the vessels are fully yielded to His operations.

YEARNING FOR WHAT THE FLESH CAN'T CONTROL

This generation yearns for that which the flesh cannot control—namely the supremacy of the rivers of God—flowing from the throne room into the hearts and eventually into the pews of our churches, streets, town squares and every home where the name of the Lord is mentioned.It is a hunger for **Christ-centeredness**. The rejection of human influence, which tends to twist the gospel into a comfort and sleepy-dozed tranquilliser for a weak people.

These young men and women desire a pure, Spirit-filled, life-transforming, and sword-piercing message that penetrates the hearts and innermost being of anyone who hears it, causing even the chief of all sinners—the least and the undeserving, like me—to repent and serve the living God, who demands to be Lord over our whole being and possessions. What love!

The hunger birthed in the bosom of our generation will make a true seeker of God recognise and acknowledge as inferior and unfulfilling anything which tries to replace or compare itself to the excellency of knowing the Son of God—His crucifixion, glorification, and second coming. Only Jesus can satisfy the hunger and thirst of this generation.

He is the prime factor and light of all of our yearning. All our endeavours in this life are baseless and vanity without

Him. He alone is worthy to sit on the throne of our hearts. He alone is to be praised, worshiped and adored forever and ever.

I pray this outpoured burden of mine will not remain only in the mind and on the shelves of the reader, but a fire will be kindled in the hearts of everyone who sincerely seeks the Lord to know His grace and to see His face.

May the Lord keep us on our knees and with our pure hands raised, together with sincere tears in our secret places, craving for that which is eternal to be established in our time as Christ is Glorified.

WE DARE NOT UNDERRATE OUR FATHERS

I once again courteously and attentively highlight the fact that this is not a manuscript to undo the goodness and the life our fathers have produced through their walk with the Lord, but it is a call to this new generation to build on the good tidings they taught us, and undo that which was only birthed by cultural influence and traditions of men.

Our fathers are the foundation and we dare not speak evil nor underrate their Christian influence on us, the younger generation. Their obedience to the Lord is the road map upon which we are to walk, their endeavours are the stepping stones for us to go further.

Notwithstanding, we cannot stay at ease. We have the moral imperative to pursue the Lord and find Him for ourselves, in order to leave a legacy for the subsequent generations too. We, as well, will also eventually become fathers of many nations—fathers of generations to come—and therefore *every step of our walk with the Lord counts.*

CRAVING TO BE TAUGHT ACCURATELY

These hungry people are in need of the Word of God and we crave and desire to be taught accurately in the knowledge of the Scriptures, that we may not become the prey of Satan and his demons. He has no new deception method, but in every generation and in different seasons, he reformulates the same three old lies initiated to man in the Garden of Eden *(Genesis 3; Matthew 4; 1 John 2:16).*

He is a master player in recycling these deceitful proposals, to sway the heart of generations from God. He presents them in a more sparkling, tolerant, acceptable language and outlook in order to attract our souls. Satan knows how prone we have become to his lies since man fell, therefore he runs about seeking whom to devour.

In the face of this critical issue, a generation must be pointed to the only solution to this dilemma—Jesus Christ—the Son of God. He alone can save us from this atrocity and from the hands of this cunning fallen angel, whose end will be eternal damnation together with his demons and false prophets, who have infiltrated the Church.

Their purpose is to twist the true Word of God and to move away the heart of God's people from the real light and love of God, which are in His son Jesus. Our generation cannot be ignorant concerning the schemes of the devil. We have the prime obligation to stay in the Word, the message of the Kingdom of God that can save our souls.

It is this same Word, preached and taught and practised by Jesus and his disciples. This generation desires to be fed by these same eternal Words, which the early church and our fathers have faithfully kept. This hungry generation has no intention to innovate, renew or adjust the Word of God to fit in any culture, tradition or trend in any society. But we are to keep that which has been handed on to us uncompromisingly.

This is the gospel of the eternal Kingdom of God and it is powerful enough to save and deliver every generation, tribe, nation, tongue and custom. It needs no touch of man to improve it. Whoever will continually believe and put his faith in the person of Jesus—Who is the prime protagonist of the Bible—will be saved.

FANNING THE FLAME

This generation is characterised as a troop in the army of the Lord of Hosts, who carry in their hands the powerful double-edged Sword of the Spirit to pull down strongholds of the enemies, set captives free to become bond slaves of the Lord. The Lord who will leave no stone unturned will also leave no territory to the domain of darkness in our time. This same Jesus, the eternal God we look to.

To such young men and women—I reach out to you—that we will continue to avail ourselves completely to Him and become the very instruments He designed as His earthly representatives. People will once again know that man was created for the sole purpose of revealing God in heaven and Jesus Christ His only begotten son, the only one through whom salvation is revealed to all creation.

It is a blessed generation which will continue to fan the flame and ceaselessly pray and study the Scriptures with their brethren. The eternal Word of God will be their daily bread and they will be purged of the worldly views and ideas that have been secretly smuggled into the Body of Christ. I am amazed by the number of youth and young adults in churches today who have no intention of serving in the Body of Christ.

GROWING IN SPIRITUAL MATURITY

It is in their local place of worship that they can be properly fed with the Word of God, taught the ways of God in order to grow spiritually and become faithful servants of God. We must be available and give ourselves to God. I pray that God may give us grace and show us mercy as we decide to serve in His Kingdom.

> "The believer and the Church are not supposed to have a better yesterday. It is supposed to be a better present and tomorrow. If our best is in the past, then we are journeying into degradation and decline, and this will eventually lead to the spiritual death of both the believer and the Church.
>
> This is not the doing of the Lord. Let our presence in the Body of Christ change the tide, that we may pour our lives and hearts into the younger generation causing an ever-continuous flow of the Spirit of God in our vessels. The convictions we sustain today are to be purified and solidified by the Lord in our circumcised hearts in order to leave a weightier foundation for our sons and daughters.
>
> Let us not end in the grave with the grace invested by God upon us but let us walk the walk of faith and leave a true legacy

behind. May the Lord cause our voice to be heard even when our time on this planet expires."

This is a final phrase from a preacher I listened to years ago that overwhelmed my heart. It still resonates in me anytime I wake up from my sleep. It is a call to my generation to decide and take a stand for God and His Church.

Chapter 2

An Urgent Word For The Body of Christ

The message of the Kingdom of God is primarily about a Saviour and King called Jesus Christ, His will and purposes are eternally planned and forever to be established not only in the heavens but as well as on earth. It is also about the corrupted nature of mankind in his sinful state because he constantly rebels against His Maker.

This man is redeemed freely by God, Who offers His only Son at the altar of sacrifice, the cross of Calvary. This same man is called to abandon his will and embrace the desire of His King and the Kingdom.

A RETURN TO THE APOSTLES' DOCTRINE

The Church must return to the purity of the preaching and teaching of the apostles' doctrine. The Church has the authority given to her—by Jesus Himself—to make disciples and teach what He taught them *(Matthew 28:18-20)*. She has the prime obligation to present the fullness of the message of the Kingdom of God, which stands totally on the Person of Jesus Christ the Son of the living God.

His birth, life, suffering, death, resurrection, and second coming—everything that He taught the apostles—is to be made known. "According to the Scriptures" or "exactly as Scripture tells it," is what must flow from our pulpits, and not the crafted, devised intelligent ideas of men *(1 Corinthians 15:3-8)*. Only in the Word is the power of God *(Romans 1:16)*.

The apostle's doctrine cannot be secondary to any other matter, topic, programme or social trend. When the Church began, Doctor Luke told us that the early believers gave themselves to what the apostles taught *(Acts 2:42)*. This is the main reason why they were a moving and vibrant movement, not a dead and cold one.

THE CHURCH IS NOT CALLED TO BE WORLD FRIENDLY

They committed their lives to the teachings of the apostles. Today if the Church would do the same thing and not rely on our own strategies, the Lord will give us more grace, show us mercy and His Word will prevail.

The Church is not called to be world friendly or to politicise her duty. She will then fail and have to compromise this holistic assignment. Instead, she must be continually filled with the Spirit of God and be purged by the blood of her Bridegroom.

In this generation, I believe the Church of God must go beyond her comfortable and well-furnished closed-door auditoriums with all her beautiful adornments and angrily face the darkness that swallows the weak outside in the world with the power and authority bestowed upon her in the name of the Lord Jesus.

The devil is appearing as a shining light, deceiving and destroying families, friends, loved ones, and our society; therefore, we can no longer afford to be tranquil while everything around us sinks. He has successfully intruded into the lives of many, using occultic practices and cunning teachings, which seem charming and fulfilling to this modern society.

THE FIGHT FOR OUR GENERATION

He presents a temporary comfort, satisfaction, and relief—but with the ultimate goal to steal, kill, and destroy God's image, that is, man. He preys on the innocence of people. He has nothing good to offer, for only God is the source of all that is good and adds no sorrow.

The Church must wake up and seek God, that He may release upon His people the Spirit of supplication and intercession to fight for our generation—to preach boldly the message of the Kingdom of God and stop the advancement of the kingdom of darkness. Notwithstanding any opposition, the Church must arise and uncompromisingly proclaim the sole truth: that Jesus is the only Saviour and the only way to God.

It is a challenge to take such a stand in our multicultural and multi-religious world, but that is the truth, and it must be preached. Truth is a Person, and His name is Jesus. Everything outside of Him is temporary, weak, and will ultimately crumble into nothing. Man cannot but build his life only on the solid rock, which is Christ Jesus, the only true Son of God.

THE POTENCY OF THE GOSPEL

Indeed, denying our selfish ambitions, aims and goals for the Kingdom of God is a heavy duty for the preacher to present. He is likely to lose a whole congregation or be tagged as an outdated spokesperson for God.

The potency of the gospel is in the full acceptance and practice of the Word of God, in which mankind is called to a higher and deeper walk with God. Man is the essential tool for the expansion of the Kingdom of God on earth, and only man can give access for the spiritual realm to invade this physical atmosphere.

Our generation, therefore, needs to be totally dedicated—spirit, soul and body—to the Kingdom assignment in these last days. This assignment was given by Jesus to His Church. We are not called to be innovative or to perfect the foundational work that the early apostles laid for us. Rather, we are called to build upon it, with the proper materials *(1 Corinthians 3:10–11).*

There is no such thing as a *progressive* Church in terms of doctrinal teachings. The Church today is not called to renovate its methods to suit the trends and mentality of the current world system in order to be acceptable and all-inclusive. Jesus the Saviour has died for all, and whoever believes in Him will be saved.

No person is excluded or required to perform any extra duty in order to enter the Kingdom of God or gain God's favour, but only to believe in the perfect sacrifice of Jesus, the Son of God, on the cross of Calvary to take away their sins.

HIS PROMISE TO EMPOWER THE CHURCH

The gospel message will prevail if the Church will depend totally on the Scriptures guided by the promptings and the leadings of the Holy Spirit, and not by her own invented initiatives. As we believe, trust and obey the Word of God, by taking the responsibility given to us by Jesus *(Matthew 28:18-20; Acts 1:8),* He will fulfil His promise, by empowering the Church to stand in times of trouble.

The Word of God is the source of true life and it is by the Holy Spirit that we can understand and interpret it rightly to save the lost soul and also to edify the believer. It is our daily guide and bread. The Holy Spirit exalts and reveals Jesus, and He will never contradict the Scriptures. Therefore, the Church's prime duty is to exalt and reveal Jesus to the listener.

Outside the Holy Spirit—Who is the Giver of Life—is falsehood, deceit, manipulation, control and temporary satisfaction, which will ultimately lead the soul to condemnation. Only in the name of Jesus and in His blood can we find salvation, healing, deliverance, restoration, true life, reconciliation, wisdom and true rest.

The full redemption plan of God must be presented without the influence of our culture and tradition. Neither should the politics of our times dictate to the Church of God what and how she should speak about the Kingdom of God and its message. The concept of self-help must be removed and abolished from our pulpits, for it is an insult to the sacrifice of the cross—Jesus shedding His own blood to atone for our sins.

Chapter 3

Man cannot Save Himself

Man in himself and by himself cannot do anything to save himself or to please God. We are all rebels and only by the grace of God are we saved, and also only by this same grace can we live to please Him. It is a society of do it yourself, and has in some way infiltrated into the mindset and conversation of certain believers.

"You shall be as God," said by the serpent, still prevails in our season *(Genesis 3:4–5)*. It is an attempt to deviate man from his source of help and make us enemies of our Creator. A generation is under the yoke of self-idolatry, self-aggrandisement, self-exaltation, self-image, and self-obsession. A confused generation searching for her identity in herself and in things rather than in Christ.

In Him is our true realisation, identity, and security. It is a self-deluded generation, and only God can save us. Many are seeking the knowledge of the divine—unfortunately, through non-biblical means—and the Church must arise in such perilous times to direct the heart of a generation to the only true way to the spiritual world, which is Christ Jesus.

PARTAKERS OF HIS DIVINE NATURE

Many are entangled in their pursuit of a sort of revelation, enlightenment and inner peace which is devoid of God and His Christ. It is a path that seems right but leads to the destruction of the soul. The Holy Spirit is the only source of true inner peace, revelation and illumination.

Any spiritual item attained outside the Holy Spirit is demonic. It may satisfy the soul of the seeker for a while, but it will definitely destroy the life of whoever trespasses this boundary. Whoever seeks to be equal with God or attain any divine life or state of being in himself or by any means is violating a divine principle, which will ultimately lead such an individual into the dark world.

Our merciful Saviour by His own blood has paved the way for every man to inherit the Kingdom of God and to be partakers of His divine nature. We are not called to be equal with Him. It is a hungry generation which needs proper guidance in order to know God, approach Him and do His will.

It is an emptiness we try to fill, a void that hunts us to seek for something beyond our human reach. It is the God-void, and He only can occupy that space in our hearts. It is a deep cry in the soul of my generation and the Church cannot keep quiet, but to explain to us what it is, and subsequently tell us what and how to deal with the situation.

It is a yearning to worship, to commune, to fellowship with someone. It is an eagerness to embrace man's only desire and purpose of living. This generation desires the supernatural and the Church has the obligation to show us the right and proper way, lest we perish.

FAITHFUL SPIRITUAL LEADERS ARE URGENTLY NEEDED

Faithful spiritual leaders are urgently needed in this season of time to lead and build up the younger generation that we may be edified and properly trained in the things of God. The apostolic doctrine is needed in the Church today, to bring us back to God and take us deeper into His ways and bring balance to a confused generation who hungrily desire God.

Many wolves have crept into the sheepfold and they are destroying the sheep and God's purpose for their lives. Therefore, fathers are once again *urgently* needed to bring the rod of God into His house that they may straighten the crooked ways and chase away the false teachers.

The authority given to the Church by her Groom Jesus Christ must be evident in all its genuineness and glory. The influence of worldly politics and human philosophy must be halted and only the Word of God must reign in our circle.

The principles of God and the sound principles of Jesus and His apostles must take their due place, and only that should be presented to the souls of men that they may put their anchor in the truth and power of God and not in the wisdom of men.

The Church is greater, and by nature, she is as eternal as her Groom, Jesus—who is constantly purifying, cleansing, and empowering her through the generations, until the day He finally comes for her in glory. Hallelujah!

In this season of deep distress and spiritual contamination, it is the responsibility of the Church of God to arise to her rightful position and take her responsibility as the arm and rod of God on earth. We must declare without any apology to the brethren and society, the non-negotiable truth of God, given to us in the Bible.

IF THE CHURCH IS TO SURVIVE THESE END TIMES

It should be clear and without ambiguity when the priest stands to declare what the Lord says. Words of truth, love, and righteousness must be made known. Everything must be weighed and balanced on the scale of the Word of God *if both the Church and the believer are to be accurate and survive these end times.*

All our intentions, plans, and objectives must have their epicentre in the infallible Word of God. It is the only reliable source on which we can build anything durable and godly. The accuracy of our belief systems and doctrine depends solely on the Scriptures, which have been inspired by the Spirit of God, Who never errs and is never out of date.

We today are not the first to experience and engage the godly life and all its expositions made available. God in diverse times and in different generations has made Himself known and made covenants with our fathers. By these covenants we are to walk in order to remain faithful to Him. As a church and individuals, our experiences are not greater or more reliable than the written Word of God.

WE MUST REMAIN ON THE SOLID ROCK OF CHRIST

No human or church organisation is therefore superior to what the canon of Scripture has already affirmed, concerning the Christian faith. The Body of Christ will be safe and at rest as far as we remain on the solid rock—our Lord Jesus Himself—the protagonist of the Bible. He is the only assurance of the Church .

There is no other safe ground on earth and in the heavens on which the Church can rely upon. The love letters He has given to us must be cherished, embraced and obeyed as our guide—to live the purposeful life—He has ordained for us all. It is His heart's dream that all men may know Him and have fellowship with Him.

Finally, this current generation looks up to the Church for moral guidance, therefore, we must live by example. Anyone who calls on the name of the Lord must practice what he preaches. The Church is the life and the light of society, so she can't afford to live a hypocritical life, a life devoid of the conviction of God.

THE FRUITS & NOT JUST THE GIFTS

Our actions are an open epistle to the world. James 1:22 reminds us to be doers of the Word and not hearers only. God seeks the fruit in us, not the gifts alone. My burden is that the Body of Christ today will rise to her feet and consciously hold the hands of the younger generation—in prayer, in the study of the Word, and in true fellowship. We are sons of the light, and therefore we cannot continue to be hidden under a basket, lest darkness prevails.

CHAPTER 4

The Call to Seek God Afresh in Every Season

In every generation, the Spirit of the Lord hovers over the hearts of men, and He desires to reveal to them the current emphasis of His dealings and projects. If we rely on yesterday's manna and fail to seek God enough, nothing significant in the Spirit will be revealed to us—and our generation will be overtaken by darkness.

Men are to seek God at all times in order to be delivered from the bondage of familiarity. A Christian can be under this yoke, which is caused by his own culture or by his familiarity with practices that have been traditionalised in his society. The man whose walk with God created the pathway and blueprint for all believers is Abraham, the father of faith.

He was called by God to leave his country, family, father's house, to the unknown, a Promised Land, a place where God had prepared for him, a new land. This was a call to abandon his comfort, security, culture and heritage to embrace the unknown. It was a new season in his life and every move and decision from that particular moment was to be birthed eagerly from a heart willing to seek God and His direction.

ABRAHAM BECAME CULTURELESS

Abraham couldn't be presumptuous in this journey. Total commitment and loyalty were required *(this is the everyday life of a believer today)*. He was culture-less, and all his dealings with God—and his obedience to Him—would now form and become the new culture: a godly culture, an unprecedented one for him, his family, and all who were in his loins—the sons of Abraham today.

Our calling is a higher one. We are called out of our culture, and God demands total obedience if we truly want to walk with Him—just like our father Abraham did. Abraham identified this God through different names, manifestations, and encounters; so will we, in different seasons and times of our lives, as we walk with Him.

Culture and tradition make people fail to take a different look at the multifaceted God of heaven. As a veil it mostly limits the vision of Christians, making them unable to embrace the God who takes people to the extra mile and breaks the boundaries of their limitations. Culture and tradition are not evil in themselves, but God will strip off every familiar thing that hinders the growth of his people and make them His fully purchased bride.

Not all who are circumcised physically are sons of Abraham, Scripture says. But even the Gentiles, who by faith believe in the Son of God. God has broken the boundaries, male and female, Jews and Greeks, free men and slaves, the circumcised and uncircumcised. We are now of a *heavenly-culture,* where the hearts of men are circumcised, men of the spiritual circumcision. These are devoid of their earthly limited traditions. A people set apart for God Himself.

THE INTRUSION OF HEAVENLY CULTURE

At the wedding in Canaan, Jesus turned the water in the pot into wine. It was their tradition to fill those pots to wash the feet of visitors, nevertheless, Jesus went beyond the cultural practice by telling them to serve the wine from those very pots. It was for cleansing, not for drinking! *He defiled their tradition in order to reach to their need.*

Neither the wedding planner nor the couple knew where the good wine came from. Indeed, it was the intrusion of the heavenly culture—where only good things dwell—into the realm of earthly culture, where men are limited. This was an introduction to a new season on earth, where men were presented before a heavenly being born on earth to manifest the heavenly culture, which is superior to the traditions of men. A new season had arrived, and man could literally see God.

Chapter 10 of the book of Acts records the first entrance of the Gentiles into the salvation plan of God. The Apostle

Peter, in this exciting passage, couldn't understand the times and seasons. According to heaven's calendar, it was time for the Gentiles to be introduced into the redemption camp of God. Nevertheless, the head of the apostles—being a Jew—was trapped by his own culture.

He refused to kill and eat from a set of animals presented to him by the Lord in a trance while praying. He couldn't go beyond his upbringing—his culture, a tradition he dearly held to—even though it was the Lord Jesus Himself commanding him. He was rebuked, even after the third time: a godly man, blinded by his own customs.

Times had changed, and a new era had begun. God had moved to another level, and men found it difficult to reach Him. Unlike Peter, the Apostle Paul would later embrace this challenge fully. By the grace of God—he being the least among them—Paul would excel at presenting the good news to every tribe and language, notwithstanding their culture.

LETTING GO OF BLINDFOLDED TRADITIONS

This is the doing of the Lord, who desires a generation that will forgo their very cherished—yet blindfolded tradition—in order to understand the seasons and times to seek after God and His desire for His Kingdom on earth.

In my short walk with the Lord as a youth, I have come to the conclusion that our faith as Christians is not an idea, a philosophy, or a set of good moral principles, nor is it rooted in a local or global religious organisation. Our faith is in a person—Jesus Christ, the eternal Son of God.

His Word is His life—and the only truth and life—for anyone who believes in Him, seeks Him, and lives to please Him. His are the only words with eternal promise, attainable only to those who seek, find, and keep them. These are the doers of the Word, not mere hearers deceiving themselves.

However, anything said or composed and practised in the Church of God by any man, which is contrary to the Word of God, must be totally rejected and kept away from the ears and hearts of believers; for it is a poison to the soul of the children of God.

RELIGION IS MAN'S ATTEMPT TO REACH GOD

Religion is what man builds in his attempt to reach and to please God. Religion is what kills the true spirit of Christianity. It is man's effort, wisdom and man's solution. Jesus rather came to reveal an eternal Kingdom, its King and the principles of that Kingdom life. Such is the initiative of God Himself.

Therefore, Christianity is the revelation of God to mankind. It is more than a religion. *Grace and faith are the means and mode of operating in this Kingdom.* It is God's enterprise—His plan, His resources, and His solution—the only one tested and approved in every generation. The principles of our faith are outlined in the Holy Scriptures, and they are made alive to every person who believes them, by the Holy Spirit.

In the absence of the Spirit of God, anything said, practised, or taught in a church in the name of God is empty words and therefore has no eternal power to change the hearts of men, nor to save their souls. Any ideology or philosophical lifestyle introduced into the Body of Christ as a way of life, which has no bearing in the Scriptures or inspiration of the Holy Spirit, will eventually bound the soul of the hearers and doers.

The Words of our Lord Jesus are to be preached, taught and practised in its fullness unashamedly regardless of the culture, tradition and background of the people. They are the only real substance of our faith. They are to be fully embraced as the basis of our living. The only true foundation of every believer under the sun.

CHAPTER 5

Growing into The Very Image of Christ

Even though I grew up in a Christian home, I found it very difficult to understand the life of a believer—the life which is fully described in the Scriptures according to God. I knew generally about the Christian religion and many of its practices and customs, but my expectation in observing many people's character and life outcomes gave me a wrong impression

Their convictions and decisions seemed to contradict the messages of the gospel I heard and read from the pulpits and in the Bible. I wondered if it was another gospel, another Jesus, and another spirit responsible for such inconsistencies.

Much of the gospel seems to be preached to take care of our temporal human needs—especially emotional and psychological issues—while the great eternal purpose of God fades away in the eyes of many believers. The power in the name of Jesus is assumed to be limited to a few issues, while important themes like the business of the Kingdom of God—to name just one—are believed to be handled only by some few elects in the church.

I KNEW SOMETHING WAS MISSING

It almost dawned on me that world affairs had more weight in influencing the minds and lives of many believers I saw around. It was when I began to dive gradually into the Scriptures that I knew something was missing, and my preoccupation from that very moment was to single out the root cause of this dilemma.

My little mind failed me numerous times as I wandered about, seeking answers. Surely, the Lord saw my heartache, and I believe He miraculously intervened by progressively opening my heart as I unhurriedly continued longing for Him—more and more—in prayers and in the Word. By His grace I was given another ear to hear what the Spirit of God has always been ministering to His Church.

DOING THE WORD OF GOD

Midweek services for Bible studies and prayer meetings became urgent appointments I could no longer afford to miss. A new and profound perception, I reckon, was mercifully granted to me as I paid proper attention to the messages from my spiritual father.

On many occasions, I felt heavy loads taken away from my heart, as I sometimes wept bitterly—without knowing the reason—both during the meetings and at home, as I meditated on the Scriptures and in my private prayers.

John 14:21 was no more a mere verse of Scripture to me, but a stream of river and a pure mirror. I got to understand that the key to the whole Christian living was exclusively *"DOING" the WORD OF GOD.*

BRINGS REAL GROWTH

A man can be part of the Church and be involved in every activity therein, he or she may even hold titles, positions and great recognition among the congregation, but if they neglect practising the Word of God, all their endeavours are a waste.

Doing what the Word of God says is the ultimate proof of love and the only way the inner man of the believer can **grow into the very image of Christ.** The individual who receives God's Word and does them is the very person who will be loved by the Father and the Son.

The manifestation of the person of Jesus in the life of the believer is a result of the person's intimate communion with the Spirit of God. Putting on the Christian name or title, and knowing the songs, practices, and all the necessary rituals is of no value if Christ is not seen in the believer.

THE NEW MAN IN ME WAS ACTUALLY GAINING GROUND

All of a sudden, I felt I had found something I was looking for. My heart was now flooded with joy and I couldn't stop loving the Lord. Right in the midst of the joy was something I'd never expected, first of all a new deep hunger and thirst for the Lord, and at the same time a great dissatisfaction for this earthly life and all the things it offers. My nights became moments of tears and groaning, as I felt the presence of God in my room.

My life spent so far occurred to me as a chase towards emptiness and vanity. I knew how deeply Christian religious cultural practices had invaded my mind and environment. There was no area in my life that I knew was intentionally and totally surrendered to the person of Jesus—even though I knew portions of the Bible, the great old godly hymns, and the attitude expected to be displayed in Sunday services. I found myself in deep darkness.

In the subsequent months I felt something was gradually dying in my being, and the more I sought the Lord, the more *I recognised the new man in me was actually gaining ground.* A new consciousness was being built up and I could see the Lord's hand in it.

A NEW SEASON HAD BEGUN

As a new born baby I could only express my inner yearning in tears to my Heavenly Father. I reckoned it was *a new season* the Lord had introduced into my life, and I had to desperately seek Him, lest I remain the same forever.

Farmers act according to the times and seasons. There is a time to sow seed, and a time to water and prune, if need be—but above all, there is also a time for the harvest. Each season requires a specific and delicate activity, which is to be implemented with particular tools and instruments by the farmer.

The weather and the atmospheric conditions can also push the farmer to adapt specific methods. Every season is essential to him, and every instrument that needs to be applied is vital and indispensable, lest he apply a wrong strategy or an inappropriate tool. A wise farmer is always ready and sober, to execute the proper operation at the set season. This makes him an adequate and productive worker.

NEVER BORING OR STATIC

As I was meditating on the Word of God one afternoon, this was an illustration I perceived in my heart concerning the life of a believer. It is a continuous and dynamic life experience with the Lord. *Never boring nor static.*

The Scriptures may give few paragraphs and pages on the lives of men and women like Abraham, Moses, Joshua, David, Sarah, Deborah, Paul, Timothy, Mary the mother of Jesus and Mary Magdalene, just to name a few.

Nevertheless, deep in every letter of those words, is the in-breathed power of the Holy Spirit that expressed the heartfelt longing of people who were sincerely hungry for God and sought Him diligently in their time. *They knew God and they walked with Him.* Men and women who preferred the chastening of a Holy God to the comfort of sin and earthly satisfaction. Their hearts were in search for God and God alone.

I desire that my generation will not be carried away by any mundane thing but to seek continually until He manifests Himself in and through us. None of the riches and glory of this age can be compared to the excellency of knowing Him and beholding His face continually.

THE HEARTFELT CRY FOR MY GENERATION

I will cry from the top of the mountains and in the lowest valleys, for my generation to follow the Saviour relentlessly, with our hearts in full assurance of faith – knowing very well that His dealings in us by the Holy Spirit at this present time are ultimately to conform us completely into the very image and likeness of Jesus Christ, the Begotten One.

Culture and tradition will have no influence in the lives of the people *pursuing hard after God.* Such people will not be limited by their traditions. The pursuit of knowledge and the secularisation of our society will not pollute the pure waters flowing from the bellies of our generation. Self and its ambitions will be done away with by the power of the cross constantly applied, in our lives.

Satan and his demons will be no match because of the mercies of God revealed in this season, and our full realisation of the authority delegated to us as believers in the name of Jesus. We shall once again be called the people of God, and the world will notice and bow its knee to the name of Jesus Christ.

CHAPTER 6

Every Generation Needs A Fresh Fire

I do pour out from the depth of my spirit that which the Lord has made a burden upon me for my generation—people like me, who, after carefully observing our uncountable religious activities and participating in numerous church programmes, still yearn and cry in their closets for the manifestation of the Spirit of God within themselves and in the churches of the living God.

More programmes have been held in the last decades than any other historical period in church calendars, with the good intention of drawing people closer to God—such as revival and awakening weeks, as well as outdoor outreach to evangelise to the lost in the world. There is nothing more noble than such organised activities for the churches of God on earth.

Nevertheless, in these few pages, I cry out for a deeper hunger for God in our secret chambers, where the pure flames of individual fire are kindled by the Lord before the corporate Body is gathered together for a higher assignment.

THE GREATEST CHALLENGE OF MY GENERATION

This is the greatest challenge for my generation, as everything seems to be legitimately seeking our attention, causing us to neglect the art of having a personal, deeper, heart-to-heart relationship with the Spirit of God, and of getting to know His ways and agenda for this present time. We are distracted by many other things.

I by no means intend to compare this generation with the past. Since their walk with God has had a great impact on our lives and influenced our culture. Nevertheless, I am sure that old flames normally need to be rekindled now and then and every generation needs a fresh fire.

A generation must know Him for themselves, since He is unsearchable and an up-to-date God. *One who is, who was and is to come.* His ways and moves are unpredictable and no man or group or generation can fully comprehend Him or put Him in a box.

Based on this very notion, I am deeply convinced that His mercies are new every morning and we today must seek to find Him. Failure to do so, will cause the darkness of this present age to blind the eyes and minds of that generation, leading them to miss the move of God in that very moment.

ENDLESS CHURCH PROGRAMMES—NO LONGER ENOUGH

Attending church meetings and programmes isn't enough anymore. Being born into a Christian cultural society does not translate to one knowing and wanting to walk with God. In fact, it is often the case that societies built on a strong Judaeo-Christian background begin to trivialise this awesome heritage

God has lost His place in the framework of their thinking; He has been kicked out of their institutions and hearts; thus, the subsequent generation desires Him no more. He is rather seen and perceived as a threat to progress and success. He is shunned at; the churches are empty and His Word is now a byword to their ears. How fallen such societies have become.

My generation has almost no experience of who God is and what He can do for the hearts of men. Meanwhile, we have heard much about Him from the pulpits. We have read a lot of books, which in some way have helped us grasp a general knowledge of Him.

Even testimonies from the older generation have, in some way, edified us—but we have not personally known this God for ourselves. This is the challenge and burden we carry: to know Jesus, and to let Him be seen, heard, and touched through our human vessel. This is true Christianity!

SHAPED BY OUR PERSONAL ENCOUNTERS WITH GOD

I seek to encourage my generation to desire to know God, just as the men and women did whose life experiences are recorded in detail throughout the Holy Scriptures. Upon careful observation, there was no area of their lives that was not shaped by their personal encounters with God.

There was no division of territory in their hearts, where God did not eventually conquer, as they surrendered their lives to Him. As a result of this, the totality of their being was transformed by such personal encounters and communion with Him. *It is still possible today!*

The very presence of the Holy Spirit revealing the person of Jesus was strongly evident in their hearts, and it was undoubtedly manifested in their outward behaviour, private and family choices, career, relationships and interactions with their contemporaries. All who met them eventually knew they belonged to the only true God of Israel.

BORN FROM ABOVE

Primarily, there wasn't any need for them to express this "life" in a special way, on a particular day or by means of some specific religious rituals and act. God was seen through their eyes, their speech and even their passing by. Whoever came into contact with such men saw and felt that indeed these men knew God.

They were totally consumed and identified by a different culture, a heavenly one. They were men of God; they were born from above! *(John 3:3-8).*

A SHALLOW GOSPEL HAS CREPT IN

My generation will need to walk this walk to bring down darkness and all the shallow gospel that has creeped into the Body of Christ, causing internal damages and injuries to the Church of the living God, producing weak believers who peacefully and ignorantly cohabit with evil as the Kingdom of darkness gains grounds in the hearts of men, families, societies, nations and unfortunately in many Christian organisations.

We are not called by God only to receive His awesome blessings, but to seek His ways as Moses did relentlessly, with an undivided attention in prayers and through the Scriptures. Totally submitting ourselves to the whole counsel of His truth without compromise, being totally transformed into His image and becoming effective instruments and tools in our society for the purposes of the Kingdom of God to be established.

WE ARE A GENERATION SICK OF THE CLICHÉ

To such breed I surely affirm that we shall see His face if we continue desiring Him. We shall be just as He is and not be ashamed. Our world will bow to the King of Glory and He will reign. May the love of God and the sweet fellowship of the Holy Spirit keep us perpetually on fire and hungry for Jesus.

We need something greater than burdensome ritualistic and repetitive Christian activities that produce no life and fruit. To a generation sick of the cliché and empty talks of mere men who do not portray Christ nor represent the Kingdom of God.

These are inspired notes to the sons of God crying from the deepest part of their being for Jesus to shine through their vessels. To those who also long to taste of the sweetness of His fellowship and receive from Him the inner strength to face this dark world that aims to viciously suppress the gospel of Jesus.

These hungry people have no goal but the advancement of the Kingdom of God and the conformity of their heart and character into the image of Jesus their Lord *(Romans 8:29; 1 Corinthians 15:49),* Who is highly exalted *(Philippians 2:9)* and enthroned in the heaven of heavens.

Chapter 7

When Culture & Tradition Oppose the Word of God

Culture, custom and human tradition may differ from place to place and they differ from each other in their practices. They mostly give interpretation on modes of conduct and also generally vary in behaviour and moral values. They are unstable and are weak in making men upright according to the righteousness of God.

The Word of God, on the other hand, remains the same in every corner of the globe—a truth we cannot help but acknowledge. Jesus preached about the Kingdom of God in a small geographical area called Israel, but after His resurrection, He commanded His disciples to faithfully proclaim that same Kingdom message to all creation on earth.

HEART PENETRATION

Indeed, its power is unlimited and mightier than the traditions of men, making it able to penetrate the hearts of men, independent of their background. The Holy Spirit, who gives the Word to the preacher to deliver, knows how to reach its listeners. The same Word but different approach according to the hearers.

Paul will boldly declare to the Church of Corinth and Galatia as becoming all things to all people for the sake of the gospel. What this does not mean is that we are to compromise with the world and its culture in order to fit in. Paul never compromised God's Word and moral standards set forth in the Scriptures, rather he was willing to forgo traditions and familiar comforts in order to reach any audience, Jewish or Gentile.

He recognised how all men are equal before the gospel, slaves, free men, Greeks and Jews, circumcised and uncircumcised. Even though the Bible often refers to some behaviour traits and practices of certain people, yet, it does not condone any practice if contrary to the prescription of God.

The Bible is a cultural book as some may say and indeed it is. But God goes beyond our culture if it is a stumbling block to the individual.

The Kingdom of God on earth expressed through the institution of the Body of Christ is a fundamental entity to study carefully. The Church in general is a heavenly institution birthed on earth by the Lord Jesus, who is both the architect, the foundation and the builder. Members of this Body are called from different traditional and cultural backgrounds to fit into this perfect eternal organic corporation.

INFLUENCED BY THE HOLY SPIRIT

We lose our individual earthly culture to live out the heavenly one, brought into our heart by the Man from heaven, who by His Spirit infuses the consciousness of the godly lifestyle practised and influenced by the Holy Spirit. Our desires, longings and deeds are now dictated by the God of heaven who seeks to establish His domain in our hearts first, then in our environment.

The book of Revelations by the Apostle John Chapter 7 verse 9 to 10 gives the picture and the scene of the end story of this magnificent Kingdom, when men from every tribe, tongue, nation are presented before the throne of their Saviour.

The man born from above or born of God is not primarily identified by his national or tribal identity that he bears by natural birth and environment of upbringing, but first of all, such men have their garments washed by the blood, and they are possessed by the Spirit of God. This heavenly life in them is devoid of any human cultural influence and it makes them Godly inside out.

THE ZOE KIND OF LIFE

It is the life of God Himself, the Zoe life. The born-again *man* is made in the image of the Son of God, though a Bethlehemite by birth, a Nazarite by upbringing, He was the *Man* sent from Heaven. His Words and deeds were from above and they couldn't be understood by mere men because they were from a different culture, a heavenly culture. As He is, so are we on earth.

We are culture-less and homeless in this realm as our father Abraham. We are now adopted as sons and heirs of another Kingdom, the eternal Kingdom where our home is, and a great incorruptible inheritance awaits us. Therefore, our security, purpose and goal are set by our heavenly Father. Nothing in this world can satisfy our soul.

One thing we should not forget is that God prohibited His chosen people Isreal from practising or involving themselves nor their children in any tradition of the other nations. They were a people redeemed by God, chosen by God Himself, as we are today. The norms and traditional believes often times point their source to the belief system of a territory.

NOT A MUNDANE LIFE

He, being a unique God, established a heavenly practice for His people so that they might be different and not mundane. In other words, Christians everywhere today share a core belief in the God of heaven and earth, who has a unique and distinct way of dealing with the people He chooses for Himself.

Such people are predestined and sanctified and above all they are set to live a higher life far above the norm, cultural and traditional practices of men. In short, we are called to live a holy and different life, which cannot be duplicated, manipulated or understood by human reasonings and philosophies.

To the believers of our time, regardless of culture or tradition, the Word of God must be the only standard by which we measure our faith, so that we can uphold and test any way of life presented to us as a doctrine or creed.

THE DANGER OF DEFICIENT DELIVERY

Scripture is never wrong, but a deficient delivery can cause more harm to listeners than any weapon of darkness. A deficient delivery is the preached letter without any inspiration of the Spirit of God, both in the preacher and the sermon.

Culture and traditions are man-made, and are therefore subject to time, seasons, and circumstances. Thus, they are unreliable. In some sects of the Body of Christ, people are instructed to perform certain specific religious ceremonies and rituals as a means of becoming—or being introduced into—the family of believers; in simple terms, to become a child of God.

Such belief-systems are biblically wrong and they have no source in the Scriptures. It is the fruit of the culture of the people attempting to replace the truth of God's Word. These practices are fully embraced by certain traditions as belief-systems in society.

NO SUCH PHILOSOPHY

We cannot find any trace of such a philosophy in any book of the Bible, nor in the creed of the early believers, as the apostles of Jesus laid down the elementary principles of the doctrine of Christ for the churches.

Jesus Himself gave a profound illustration in the gospel of John, chapter 3, while Paul provided further clarification on the matter of being born again—or being born of God—in Romans 10:8–13.

Chapter 8

Hard Truths Our Saviour Never Hid

In the book of the Acts of the apostles Chapter 16 from verse 30 to 34 Paul and Silas answers the question of the prison guard, *"Sirs, what must I do to be saved?"* After they were miraculously released from prison by God's intervention. John in his gospel, in Chapter 1 from verse 11 to 13 talks of a group of people who *became children of God only by receiving Jesus Christ His Son.*

Peter, on the Day of Pentecost—as recorded in Acts 2:14-41—delivered the first Holy Spirit-filled sermon by the Church to all who were present in Jerusalem. When the hearts of the listeners were convicted, they asked what they ought to do regarding the Kingdom of God, and their question was answered precisely in verses 38 and 39: *"Repent and be baptised in the name of Jesus."*

THE ULTIMATE REQUIREMENT

These all provide the explicit requirement by which any human being, born of a woman, must to do willingly in order to enter the Kingdom of God. It is not an idea established by any preacher or famous religious personality nor a certain élite group of leaders, but the Son of God Himself who is the only way, truth and life.

Salvation, or becoming a child of God is not the doing of any man, neither is it an attestation or certificate handed out by any local church pastor or a group of religious leaders, but it is the Spirit of God giving faith to mankind to believe in Jesus for the forgiveness of their sins, and that man can continually and fully trust only in Jesus to the very end of his existence on earth.

This is accompanied by the indwelling presence of God in the heart of the person. As the Spirit now lives in him, He—the Spirit of God—by His eternal power, begins a supernatural work of transformation. With the cooperation of this newly born-again believer, as he feeds on the Word of God and hungers for deep intimacy with God through ceaseless prayer, the believer develops a desire for fellowship with other believers, a love for humanity as God Himself loves, and a hatred for sin and evil.

These all are visible by others as fruits on a tree, all these are the doings of the Lord in the life of any true child of God. After all, no man can come to Jesus, if the Father doesn't draw him *(John 6:44)*. These are the solemn and ever truthful words written in the Bible by the inspiration of the Holy Spirit to all humanity. Who dares modify or change them!

A RETURN TO CLEARER BIBLICAL DOCTRINE

It is a hard truth but certainly worth teaching in the Body of Christ today. Issues concerning the person of Jesus as the only author of salvation, His deity, humanity and Lordship, as well as the only One to whom our prayers and services are to be directed. In His name we are instructed to pray to the Father and only on His name we are to call in times of trouble and also for our daily needs.

The Church must also return to the teachings on the sinful nature of man—his total, irreversible depravity and corruption without exception—and on Jesus being the only answer provided by God to this dilemma.

These teachings include God's plan of redemption; the Holy Spirit as an eternal Person, not a mere symbol; His present ministries on earth; the reality of heaven and hell; and the non-existence of purgatory, as believed in certain religious groups.*"And it is appointed for men to die once, but after this the judgment" (Hebrews 9:27 NKJV).*

In some religious cultures, it is believed that every deceased person has departed to be with God. The dead only needs a prayer and a religious burial in order for his or her soul to be accepted by God in heaven, where he or she will have an eternal rest.

WHEN CULTURE INFILTRATES THE TRUTH

Though it is a message intended to bring comfort and relieve the pain of the bereaved in a grievous and devastating moment, it remains a religious cultural belief that has infiltrated the Body of Christ—one that is contrary to the truth presented in the sermons of Jesus and the Apostle Paul in the Scriptures. Paul spoke about those who are dead *in the Lord* in 1 Thessalonians 4:13–18.

The term *in the Lord* in the Scriptures refers to people who are born of the Spirit of God, those who repented of their sins and continued to trust in Jesus Christ as their Lord and Saviour, while they lived on earth.

Revelation 20:11–15 gives a broader perspective. The throne mentioned in this passage is **not** the throne where believers are rewarded for their service, for different crowns—and therefore different rewards—will be given to each believer according to his or her faithful work for the Kingdom of God on earth. Those rewards are for believers in Christ Jesus and are earned through their work, which is empowered by God's grace, enabling them to fulfil specific tasks and assignments for His Kingdom on earth.

HARD TRUTHS JESUS TOLD OPENLY

Salvation is not a reward but a free gift from God to all who believe in Jesus as specified in Ephesians 2 verse 8 to 9. The scenario in Revelations rather presents all kinds of people standing before the throne of God to be judged either to eternal rest or to eternal condemnation.

If everyone were guaranteed free passage and everlasting rest with God, there would be no reason for this picture of the final reckoning. In the gospels, Jesus spoke explicitly about the two destinies that await all mankind after we leave this earth.

The story of the rich man and Lazarus in Luke 16 contains the foundational teaching of Jesus regarding the two destinies of all people after death. Numerous other passages, both in the Old and New Testaments, also affirm the reality of the two destinies that await all humanity in eternity. Being the Saviour, *He could not hide this hard truth from us.*

HAIR-RAISING & FRIGHTFUL PORTIONS OF THE BIBLE

His gracious nature has made provision for the salvation of all mankind. Our God is both merciful and just, and nothing done under the sun is hidden from Him. The Bible says that books will be opened, and we will all be judged according to how we lived on earth—both our actions and our motivations. There will be a great separation among men, as Jesus clearly stated.

Death, hell, and the lake of fire are mentioned in these frightening passages. How dreadful it is for one's name not to be found in the Book of Life. The Church today must preach this wholesome truth to a lost world—that there is hope after this earthly life for those who believe in Jesus Christ, the Saviour of the whole world.

Our loving and gracious God has prepared a place that was never intended for man. Nevertheless, it will one day—and forever—be occupied by Satan, his demons, and some human beings whom God created in His own image and likeness. A deep cry rises within me as I read these hair-raising and frightful portions of the Bible.

The full and complete message of salvation in Jesus needs to be preached today more than ever before. How can the Church fail to proclaim the whole truth about the horrible destiny that awaits all those who reject the eternal, redemptive gospel of Jesus—His love, mercy, and long-suffering in not wanting any to perish?

WATERED DOWN & LOW STANDARD DISTORTIONS

Unfortunately, what is often presented is a watered-down, low-standard gospel that seeks to draw people away from the truth of Jesus in order to weaken the Body of Christ and to bend the mind of generations from God and His Words. It offers a false hope and a distorted reality to the hearers.

CHAPTER 9

Hungry for the Truth

Men are hungry for the truth; therefore, the Church must present this truth according to the Scriptures without taking away or adding to it. We need the Holy Spirit to help us in order to rightly divide and present the Word of God.

In certain cultures, some believers are tagged as practical Christians, these ones actively attend churches on a weekly basis or say their prayers very often and practice the teachings of Christianity.

They have earned this name among their contemporaries or they claim themselves to be so because of their active participation in Christian activities both within the Church and outside.

Meanwhile, there remains a significant group who, even though they define themselves as believers, have no intention of attending church except for significant events such as Christmas and Easter.

Reading the Word or having a private prayer life or above all a relationship with God is not their thing. The idea of having a personal relationship with the God they claim to acknowledge is odd to them. Many in these circles have never been taught to get closer to God.

NOT FOR FALSEHOODS & UNBIBLICAL SUPPOSITIONS

Having an intimacy with God or representing Him as the Apostle Paul teaches is a profession for a selected few. Reading the Bible is even a challenge. Such believers if they may be called so have no relationship with God. they are familiar with certain definite rituals and Christian events, which they solemnly observe.

A general knowledge of an existing Supreme Being does not constitute one to be a believer in biblical terms. Neither does regular church attendance make one a child of God. The Bible is very clear on this issue, but its truth has been watered down and somehow eliminated and substituted with a more inclusive view and unbiblical suppositions, which create a falsehood in the heart of men and women.

Presenting the raw truth as explicitly outlined in the Scriptures is tiresome for some preachers, but it is the only authority upon which our salvation is built. Anything outside the Scriptures preached and practised as a means to become a child of God and to enter into His Kingdom is false and must therefore be abolished totally from our pulpits.

THE VALIDITY OF SCRIPTURE IS ETERNAL

Only the Word of God stands. His Words are truth and they are life to anyone who believes and practice them uncompromisingly. Some churches derive their believes from the cultural systems of the society by doing away either totally or partially with the only true authority available, thus, the Holy inspired Scriptures written by holy men and women as the Holy Spirit moved them.

The practice of the Christian life is not something that is written in our present time by a group of religious leaders in a conclave or seminar. It is *fully decoded* by God in the Scriptures and its validity is eternal, having the power to change and influence any race of people in any given generation.

No human culture can influence or change the Bible to their pleasing or to suit their mindset. No group of religious Christian leaders have the authority to edit the Holy Scriptures to suit their unbelief and the trend in a generation. The earth and the heavens and everything in them came into existence by the powerful Word of God.

All things will pass away but only the Word of God will endure to the end. How dare mere men attempt to change it! It is an attempt unfortunately sustained and positively recommended by the devil through certain personalities in the Christian faith to reduce the potency and the reliability of the Scriptures by which men and women of every generation can know God and be acquainted with His ways.

THE RISE OF APOSTASY, HERESIES & FALSE DOCTRINES

Attacking the Scriptures is the cause of all the divisions we have so far in the Body of Christ. Right from the time of the early believers, the Apostles Paul, Peter and John warned the Churches of the rise of apostasy, heresies and false doctrines. Such teachings aim at eliminating the person of Jesus Christ and the Holy Spirit as the only foundation and power available for the Church of God on earth with the doctrine of demons and philosophies.

The Church today is more conscious of the trends in society than the prophetical position of the Holy Spirit in our time. Some Churches are seeking means to please the society through the adaptation of methods of appeasement rather than her first assignment and duty, that is to remain holy, faithfully preach the Word without compromise and equip the sheep for the harvest.

It is almost hard for the congregation to gather as one to intercede rather than for a picnic. Evangelism is assigned to a few "spiritually sound" while wedding ceremonies, birthday celebrations etc are invited by all. There is no price to pay and no sacrifice to make. A God who only gives and never requests anything from his children is the idol in which we delight ourselves today.

THE FULLNESS OF THE WORD MUST BE EMBRACED

The fullness of the Word must be embraced and we must avoid minimising the efficacy of the Word of God. The Old

Testament is as powerful as the New Testament and they are both referred to as the Word of God. Paul, Philip, Peter and the early fathers preached Christ from the Scriptures they had, which were obviously the compilation of the Old Testament.

Jesus is fully expressed through the personalities, events, feasts and names throughout the Old Testament. Our knowledge of the Word will be deficient if the Church today give little place to the life of the old saints expressed through the prophecy of Scriptures. Not even an iota or dot will pass away from the law, Jesus said.

He read concerning Himself from the book of Isaiah and reaffirmed His existence before Abraham, much more He told them how Moses had written about Him. The Word of God must be fully preached, taught and presented in the wisdom of God and in Power.

NOT TO QUENCH HEAVENLY FIRE

Any cultural or traditional practices introduced and observed in the Church as a way of life for believers, which is contrary to the Word of God should be banished from the Body of Christ and tagged as principles of men. Such principles mislead God's people, they are often times influenced by evil spirits and whispers of demons seeking access to cause damage to the believers.

No matter how good and promising they may sound or how lasting they have been proclaimed for generations, they are no match to the inspired and written Word of

God that gives life to the dead. Such practices shouldn't be permitted or introduced into the Body of Christ because they will eventually quench the heavenly fire in the hearts of the believers.

CHAPTER 10

The Authority & Power Of God's Word

The Word of God cannot be broken and will endure to the end while everything under the sun crumbles. The Word of God is our only true foundation and we must solemnly lay hold of all of it in order to remain in the Lord.

Furthermore, the New Testament believer—new creation—is born and introduced into a new culture, a divine and heavenly one, totally under the domain, influence and leadership of the Holy Spirit in their hearts.

This culture carries a totally different way of living without any stain of human or demonic ideology and influence. This culture prioritises Jesus and His Words above any other voice. The reliable Word of God, which is trustworthy from ages to ages and from generation to generation outlines the principles for living.

Men in this culture are Kingdom minded and seek nothing but the advancement of the Kingdom of God on earth, notwithstanding any opposition. The man introduced into this culture will find his meaning of existence while he humbly and obediently seeks the will of God first.

REVEALING THE PURPOSES & NATURE OF GOD

Our sufficiency, provision and every other thing we will ever need to prosecute the life He planned for us are in Him. There is nothing surer and more stable and life changing as the eternal Word of God.

A message entitled *The Authority and Power of God's Word* by Derek Prince profoundly changed my view, perception, and understanding of the Word of God. It is the only certainty and the true compendium of the reason for life on earth.

Upon this validity of truth given to mankind by the Holy Spirit through the men and women He chose as the recording instruments can we establish our lives. The Word never changes and it reveals the very purpose and nature of God to all men regardless of their nationality and background.

It is forever settled in heaven and nothing can contradict its validity. Therefore, any person who will ever live on this earth will find his or her true meaning in this life if he or she surrenders to the God of this Book, the Bible.

Our generation cannot afford to live without encountering this God and trusting on His Word. It is our daily responsibility and obligation to do so. In different seasons and generations, God revealed His purposes to men as they navigated in the Spirit to know what was incubated in the realm for their time. We ought to do the same before the darkness engulfs us.

WE LIVE IN A POSTMODERN SOCIETY

We need to be like the Berean church who searched the Scriptures in their homes after meetings. Very few do this today, and spiritual blindness is the outcome of our negligence in going deeper in the Scriptures and prayers.

We live in a postmodern society where everything is relative and there is no such thing as objective truth. Everything is defined by personal persuasion, reasoning, and human feelings. It is a society with no solid ground from which any lasting principle can proceed.

Man has made himself his own god, and gain is seen as the purpose of life. A shallow and superficial doctrine of life which paves the way for a deep darkness to prey on the younger generation, who have been left orphans and blind to choose their own path.

The Scriptures are holy, just as their Author—the Holy Spirit—is holy, and so are the men and women He used to write them. They reflect the holy nature of God and therefore cannot contain errors or inconsistencies, as some mistakenly claim. From time immemorial, they have been opposed by kings and kingdoms, yet they still stand while those kingdoms have perished.

The modern man cannot fully understand it notwithstanding his intellectual capacities. They are too deep to fathom and only the Holy Spirit can open the eyes of the reader that he may see the wondrous things eternally packed in them.

CALLED TO RELENTLESSLY SEEK THE LORD

Thank God for the foundation laid by the apostles upon which we are to build with the proper materials, as indicated in the Scriptures. Nevertheless, we are to seek the Lord relentlessly to know what and how we ought to do, in any given season and period.

His ways are unsearchable but He is willing to make them known to those who diligently seek to know His will. However powerful a man may be, his reference in teaching and expounding of the gospel must be derived from the Bible and by the inspiration of the Holy Spirit who will never contradict the Scripture.

Any person ministering the Word of God without the inspiration of the Holy Spirit will produce no life to the hearers no matter how articulate or charismatic he or she may be. It is the Spirit who gives life but the letter kills. The deliverer of God's message must receive a current breathed-in impulse from the Spirit of God in order to address any current generation.

NOT REMAIN STAGNANT & STUCK IN THE PAST

Old testimonies are great, but time makes everything fizzle out. The eternal Spirit of God is always present and is in us even now brooding and speaking in our hearts the godly realities by releasing upon us the grace to live in our time. From His bosom He unveils the agenda for this present generation.

Tradition makes us stick to the norms, glued to our know-how and makes us become slaves of the routines of men. Some religious leaders today still sustain certain past legends and myths written in some books for Christians, but are untrue and yet seek to give a perspective of what the Kingdom of God is like, and how the believer ought to live.

These are man-made framed and concocted fairy tales, which in time ceases to produce life—if it had any— but almost and always able enough to keep generations stagnant in their Christian walk.

Respectfully, observe some believers who have made no significant progress in the Lord and have failed to grow spiritually. Such people are attached to their past and to old testimonies. Their understanding of God, and the way they speak about Him, often revolves around past glories—the "once upon a time" powerful God who once did wonders.

NOT REMAIN STAGNANT [illegible] IN THE [illegible]

[illegible]

[illegible] in their Christian walk.

[illegible]

CHAPTER 11

Every Generation should Know the Lord & Walk in a Greater Dimension

As we saw in the previous chapter, it often appears that the God some people proclaim has stopped doing great works – both in them and through them. It is as if He has somehow run out of resources to advance His Kingdom purposes on earth. Such a God they highly revere, while at the same time looking down on the previous generation that was not present in their era.

NO PRAISE FOR OLD MIRACLE WORKERS

Elisha's life must be studied again. He was an ordinary farmer who left everything to serve Elijah, yet he received a double portion of his master's anointing and worked mightily in his time after Elijah's departure. Even after his death, a dead man was raised to life when his corpse touched the bones of this anointed prophet.

Surely, his God was even still alive and did an outstanding miracle even *after* his death. This is the blueprint of real Christianity, that every generation will know the Lord and walk in a *greater dimension.* We will not praise an old miracle worker and live in darkness crippled by the evil one who seems to be more updated than the sons of light.

...OR NEWER GENERATIONS THAT FAIL TO DIG NEW WELLS

Jesus, our true example, and the apostles are still remembered today because their works and toil are as eternal as the God they represented. We ought to live the same way. My generation will perish if we neglect God's Word, and nothing of eternal significance will be accomplished if we fail to keep the candlelight burning perpetually within our inner man.

If our generation fails to dig new, deep wells for fresh water, we will end up like the Samaritan woman at Jacob's well. She knew the exact location of where they worshiped and saw it as something to boast about, but she did not realise that a new Person had entered the scene—the Messiah, Jesus Christ, who is more than a Jew, more than a prophet, but the only Son of God and the Saviour of the whole world.

The real fountain of living waters had arrived on the scene and yet she was still going to draw water from an old source. The eternal inner river giver was in front of her, yet she asked Him how He was going to draw from a man made well.

OH, HOW WE NEED TO DRINK THIS FRESH WATER DAILY!

Our generation urgently needs to be re-introduced to this Lord of lords and the soon coming King. He will freely give the fresh and living waters to anyone who asks Him. Jacob's well was ok, but *behold I do a new thing says the Lord.* Jacob's well was a reference, not the standard. It is a teacher to bring us to the real person, Jesus Christ Himself. The Man sent from Heaven. Oh, how we need to drink this fresh water daily.

The Christian culture is a very important aspect for many individuals and for society at large, just as Jacob's well was to the Samaritans. She strongly believed in God, but her belief-system was forged by this very notion, just as many of us today in Western societies.

Nevertheless, this same heritage can become a hindrance—a blockage that keeps a person from pressing forward to know the true reality of Christianity: a relationship with God the Father and His Son, Jesus, by the power of the Holy Spirit. For some, it is a barrier as they enter the Kingdom of God with prejudices and misconceptions rooted in their cultural and traditional backgrounds.

HIS AGENDA & PURPOSE FOR US IS NEW & FULLY ENCODED WITHIN HIS HEART

Some Christians wouldn't attend particular local churches or serve certain ministers of the gospel because of their nationality, culture or the colour of their skin.

The Lord is not monotonous, neither is His Spirit limited by any force. He has unsearchable ways and means for each generation to cross their barriers, either by the raising of a rod, by stepping into it, by striking it with a mantle or by speaking to it. He chooses. Each generation has to seek Him for the right way.

No one can fully comprehend Him. He is a fresh God and His agenda and purpose for us is new and fully encoded within His heart. It is worth searching for. *He reveals, we act!* If young believers now fail to sincerely search the Scriptures and get into *deep intimacy* with Him, that He may open our eyes to see the wonders in them, it will be as if He never lived in their time.

There has never been a time in history when Christians had more access to the written Word of God—through apps, printed copies, and digital editions. We have an abundance of Bible translations, commentaries, and encyclopaedias, yet it seems we are becoming dull and cold spiritually.

Our heads are filled with every kind of knowledge, while our spirit man lies on the sick bed gasping for his last breath. The prophets of old were inspired to pen down a compendium of collected books, the Bible which outruns generations, giving us an overwhelming revelation of the mind of God from eternity past to eternity future.

WE MUST GO DEEPER IN HIM TO KNOW WHAT HE INTENDS FOR US IN OUR TIME!

The same eternal Spirit of God has not stopped brooding over the hearts of His people, and He is willing to open sealed revelations to those who seek Him. Just as He gave Moses specific instructions to part the Red Sea, He gave Joshua different instructions for crossing the Jordan—Joshua didn't need to stretch out a rod as Moses did, yet God still made a way for his generation.

A new way to address obstacles was needed, and as men of God for a particular generation they needed to seek the Lord to know what and how He intended to challenge them. The Lord does new things and we must go deeper in Him to know what He desires for us today in our time! God is *present*. God is *now!*

His Words are powerful and life changing. No human words or traditional principles can be compared to His. These are some few selected verses from the Word of God and what it can accomplish in a person's life:

2 Timothy 3:16-17; Matthew 7:24; 2 Peter 1:20-21; Psalm 12:6; John 10:35; Matthew 4:4; Matthew 5:17-18; John 16:12-14; Hebrews 4:12; 1 Thessalonians 2:13; Hebrews 5:12-14; Psalm 119:130; Psalm 107:17-20; Proverbs 4:20-22; Psalm 119-9-11; Psalm 17:4; Ephesians 5:25-27; James 1:21-25; John 12:47-48; 2 Peter 1:4; Romans 10:17; James 1:18; 1 Peter 1:22-23; 1 Peter 2:2.

CHAPTER 12

Power Through Prayer & Private Devotion

On the subject of prayer and personal devotion, I recommend Edward M. Bounds' manual *Power Through Prayer.* After reading this book, I felt deeply how far I had yet to go in developing a deeper prayer life with God. The Holy Spirit longs to take us into new depths, but only if we are willing to pay the price of laying aside everything to seek His face.

Time is a key factor in prayer, yet in today's hurried, fast-paced world, every aspect of life seems to demand our time. Nevertheless, we have neglected the practice of waiting on the Lord as the men and women of old once did. They knew God and had a deep relationship with this Supreme Being.

THE IMPORTANCE OF CULTIVATING AN INTIMATE RELATIONSHIP WITH GOD

We all spend time in those things we cherish most; our personal and collective priorities reveal just how little we truly hunger for God. My generation have very little interest in building and cultivating an intimate relationship with God—our heavenly Father—through prayer. For this reason we are weak and unstable even in our Christian walk.

Prayer is not a religious activity, neither is it one of the numerous prescribed religious Christian rituals in order to please God. For the believer in Christ, prayer is life. *"Men always ought to pray and not to faint" (Luke 18:1 KJV).* These are the very words of Jesus. Praying is living. It is the very air we breathe.

A believer who has no prayer life is a fainting believer, such a man is an easy prey for the devil and life circumstances. Such believers are driven to and fro by the wind of earthly issues. Men are originally designed by God as praying and communing beings. We are solely made to commune with God.

A praying man cannot be manipulated by anything that is not of God, nor can he be swayed by his current mood or feelings. In both good and bad times, he prays. For the child of God, prayer is a holy convocation, experienced primarily in the heart through the indwelling Spirit of God. All people—the rich and the poor, the healthy and the sick, the young and the old, the educated and the illiterate—are called to participate in this *heavenly communication network.*

THE FIRST DUTY OF ALL MEN IS TO PRAY

The Son of God—Jesus—lived an intense life of prayer, and we, His followers, are also called to do the same. We are commanded to labour fervently and continually in prayer. Indeed, Jesus has paid the ultimate price for our salvation and has provided all that is needed for godly living; nevertheless, it is only through prayer that these realities are manifested in our lives.

The first duty of all men is to pray. Outside of the prayer camp is darkness, confusion, futility and perdition. Men who abandon the life of prayer are like dust to the serpent. The God of the Bible is first of all a prayer answering God.

He has vowed to hear whoever calls on Him from a pure heart, and whoever diligently seeks Him. Having said this, we are not to stop hungering for Him after we have received the blessings of an answered prayer. Prayer is bigger than receiving a sincere request from God.

Praying first of all, transforms us, just as our Lord's countenance changed as He prayed on the mount of transfiguration. Secondly, as His representatives, we enact and enforce the will of our Father on earth through prayer. Furthermore, the reality of being made priests in His Kingdom is manifested when we pray.

PRAYER IGNITES & TRANSFORMS THE INNER MAN

Prayer ignites the inner man, and the old man is experientially put to death in the life of the praying believer. Meanwhile, sin sits on the throne and rules with an iron fist in the life of the fainting believer – one who has abandoned the source of power needed to live and overcome sin. Tragically, such a believer has his spiritual senses deadened, making him powerless and helpless in the sphere of temptation and trials.

We are called to live a victorious life in Christ Jesus, and this young generation must be thoroughly instructed in the art of personal, ceaseless prayer. We must be fully awake to the immeasurable resources made available by God through His Holy Spirit. In Him is our victory, joy, and all that we need.

Many are rich and gifted in the Spirit, but cannot manifest these realities bestowed on them by God, just because they refuse to labour in prayer. Prayer is foolishness to the nonspiritual and spending time with God in prayer is too hard a task for the babe in Christ.

He is only physically minded, and the things of the Spirit, which are permanent, are unreal to him. The grace for supplication and interceding for others is the ultimate gift God gives to a man. And such believers go beyond themselves in order to embrace God's compassion and love for mankind.

HE WHO STOPS PRAYING—STOPS LIVING

Love God and love your neighbour as yourself is the prime duty of all men, and praying to God and for all men is the starting point. He who stops praying, stops living, and such a man blindly delivers the keys of his life and that of others in the hands of the wicked one. God forbid!

Men will suffer in vain if they neglect prayer. Christians will live below the standard of the Christ life in them, if they stop praying. Prayer is what men bring to the table of negotiation, that God may intervene from heaven in their affairs. Since we cannot exhaust praying, God in His infinite mercies has made an abundant provision for the man, woman or child, who engages themselves in it.

He multiplies strength, wisdom and grace to whoever calls continually on Him, that we may have the stature to stand before Him and change the corse of circumstances and situations in our environment. Prayer makes us a useful instrument in the hands of our God in His Kingdom.

We spend time in our working places and we are almost always willing to do extra hours for extra money when our boss requests. We do all this to show how faithful we are to the company. We spend time at wedding ceremonies, birthdays and other social gathering and people will often request for extra hours for the party to go on.

A MONUMENT VS. A MOVEMENT

These are legitimate moments we share with families, friends and loved ones. We spend time to stay on the phone with loved ones and friends, talking about important and sometimes unnecessary issues. Social media, with its positive and negative impacts on society, also steals away much of our time—often more than we are willing to admit.

Nevertheless, an extra twenty minutes prayer by the worship leader will cause many to complain. The preacher must be quick and stick to time. Time spent in personal prayer is a strange topic for some Christians today. A man whose soul longs after the Lord knows the issue of time in personal devotion.

I by no means neglect the fact that there should be discipline and a sound use of time in all church activity. Three principles I hold to are fully illustrated in the early church life, as seen in the book of Acts: *"They continued steadfastly in the apostles' doctrine and fellowship, in the breaking of bread, and in prayers" (Acts 2:42).*

The Church today seems to be more skilful and humanly organised, *(with more sophisticated items than they had).* Nevertheless, I wonder—despite having these three basic yet fundamental principles—how theirs was a moving church, unlike ours today, which has become more of a monument than a movement.

CHAPTER 13

Fully Soaked

IN THE DEEP WATERS OF OUR PRIVATE DEVOTIONS

The power and yoke of sin is broken in this hour of prayer. It is in this moment that the Lord personally sweeps His Spirit of conviction in the heart of the believer, revealing all the hidden thoughts of the deep inward parts. Leading us to godly sorrow as we genuinely repent. It is that moment of great conviction where I have cried out my soul, knowing how dirty I am before His holy face.

The Body of Christ must sound the alarm concerning this deep intimacy with His bride. Our few hours of corporate prayer is not enough for a hungry soul; it is only when the members are fully soaked in the deep waters of their personal devotion can they benefit from the two-hour church prayer.

The preacher's sermon is anointed by this personal intimate oil he received in his secret chamber. The worship team and our song ministrations will be anointed if the singers will immerse their hearts in the deep well, to receive a fresh sound and melody from the Lord during his or her personal commune with the Spirit of God.

THE ALARMING SOUND OF EMPTY BARRELS!

So, as the Bible teacher in his exposition of the Scriptures. Unfortunately, some neglect cooperate prayers because they simply have no or little personal devotion with the Lord. When the believer ministering to the Church has no personal devotional life, those in the pew who are conscious of the Spirit of God in their heart are *alarmed.*

They perceive such display instantly, and oh how sad it is when the sound of an empty barrel makes noise in the sanctuary. Such ministration is birthed on a cold and quenched altar. There is *no fire from the Lord* and the heart of the listeners are left fruitless no matter how sweet the voice or the eloquence in his or her speech. It itches the ear and is painful to the soul.

No spiritual edification, no conviction, no transformation in the soul and no life is produced. The believer who neglects personal devotion generates no life in the assembly, no oil to give to others and no fruit for the hungry to feed on.

THE DISPLAY OF GIFTS & TALENTS CAN NEVER SUBSTITUTE INTIMACY WITH THE HOLY SPIRIT

The display of gifts and talents can never substitute intimacy with the Holy Spirit in the Church of God. Never! Such a believer has no appetite for the Word of God, no hunger for personal prayer either. He rarely calls on the name of the Lord if not in times of real physical need. His words in prayer will be a repetition of words without revelation.

His prayer will be based on his personal needs and will hardly speak on behalf for anyone outside his spectrum. Intercessory is a no-go area for such a one. Sacrifice is a foreign language and giving his all, is an abomination. Believers who minister in the Church without a personal overflow of oil, end up killing and freezing the atmosphere

They cannot bring any perspective of the Kingdom of God to the believers present. They cannot draw men to the presence of God. Neither can they host His presence. In such churches, men's activities reign rather than the Holy Spirit's. Such men need to be humbly approached, admonished, prayed for and tutored by the spiritually sound in the congregation, that he may learn to bring *fire, oil* and *edification* to the Body of Christ.

EMPTY EXHIBITIONS DON'T SET HEARTS ABLAZE

The Church is not a concert show to admire the stage man and his exhibition, neither is it a theatre to stare at a performer. It is the gathering of the holy ones of God who are set ablaze in their hearts in order to quicken the dead and weak among them.

The four gospels consistently record a particular duty Jesus practiced before daybreak: He went out to the mountainside to pray and, at times, spent the night in prayer to God. This phrase and pattern appear repeatedly throughout the Scriptures. The Son of God, full of the Holy Spirit, would not begin His day without personal devotion with His Father.

What a staggering statement. He would often choose solitude over people. This is a concept very foreign to the Church today where we a taught to be almost always with people. Indeed, we can't avoid people, we live as humans basically for one another, but this solitude with God was a moment without any interference. A moment wholly dedicated to our Creator who can't wait to share His heart with His beloved chosen children.

CONCEPTION IS THE RESULT OF DEEP INTIMACY

We are equipped and refreshed in such solitary moments. The secrets of the Lord that no eyes have seen nor ears heard or touched by any man are released to such hearts that are made available only to the Lord. Seals are broken in this space of heart-to-heart engagement. This is where the bride and the bridegroom share the deepest intimacy. It belongs to them only, as a secret avenue where conception takes place.

The beauty of this Oneness overwhelms my being when I fathom the slightest goodness of His mercy He showed me. I run into this closet and I shut the door as often as I can. It is the door of my heart and the door of my noisy distracted soul. I shut it as He quickens me. It is the best moment of my life and the precious thing He gave me. The privilege to dine with Him alone.

> I come out as a giant and my chains and flaws are always swallowed up by the power of the Holy Spirit. The day I miss Him is the day darkness overshadows me. The cost is too much to pay, therefore I will pay the price and stay at the throne room where the blood of Jesus cleanses, where I receive mercy, and His grace is poured upon me all the time. I stay there until I am fully wet and socked in His glory.

This is the first meeting place for the saints of this generation. The Christian who has no personal devotional life is a believer who has not yet surrendered totally to the Lordship of Jesus Christ. Such a believer prefers Him as Saviour from hell, sickness, doom and poverty. But to be the Lord of all the affairs of his heart, is too much.

FORGOTTEN SERMONS: SELF-DENIAL, THE CROSS & DYING TO SELF

The Body of Christ is full of such ones, making it hard for churches to go the extra mile in the pursuit of the Kingdom of God. A self-seeking set of believers are open to the preaching of *material gain* only. A message finalised to their benefit only, and never that which blesses God, even if we are the ones to lose.

Self-denial, the cross and dying to self are forgotten sermons. Nevertheless, in these are our best life encapsulated by God Himself, that we may be empty of ourselves and full of His riches to reign in this life and in the life to come with Him.

It is my deepest plea, that this generation will live their lives as burden-bearers for families, the Body of Christ, communities and nations. That which will drive them will be the purpose and will of God yoked upon them in their secret places of prayer.

As the calling of Paul into the apostleship circle was commenced by their cooperate ministering to the Lord, when the Holy Spirit told them to separate some few to that ministry. People will also find their calling when they come into the knowledge of worshipping together with the whole Body of Christ.

The neglect of this aspect of Christianity has given birth to a wave of rebellious and confused Christians who believe it is possible to live the believer's life without any connection or communion with other believers. That is a fallacy, a false mindset, devilish and dangerous.

Chapter 14

The Adventures Of the Sons of God on Earth

Every member of our physical body is attached to another member. It is one body but many and different members, just as the Body of Christ, a cooperate body. What a shame when people begin to construct their own mindset and conceptions about how Jesus built, laid the foundations and the principles of church life illustrated by Apostle Paul in his letters.

If we are humble and accept our mistakes and faults, repent and forgive one another and embrace the oneness of the Body of Christ, we can do wonders. It is not an institution of the one-man-show or the super-star, but the adventures of the sons of God on earth.

Watchers and gatemen will arise among us, to defend territories. *"I sought for a man to stand in the gap,"* as God said is this astonishing statement *(found in the book of Ezekiel).* The eternal all-powerful God waiting for the mortal man he made to give Him the permission to act. How humbling is that thought to us and how fearful we should be if we refuse to make ourselves available for Him to intervene in the affairs of our churches and territories.

> I searched for someone who would repair the wall, one who fills the gap, an intercessor to cry out for mercy, but I found no one. There was no one found who would keep my justice from destroying the nation.
>
> Ezekiel 22:30 TPT

MEN LIKE GIDEON & JOSHUA WENT BEYOND TRADITION & CULTURE TO OBEY GOD

Men like Gideon will encounter the Lord and be commissioned to pull-down family idols. He went beyond his family traditions and culture to fulfil God's promise. We ought to do the same. The Joshua generation will spy the good land promised by God and do damage to their opponents.

Weak men will meet their David in caves and they will be godly—trained as mighty men—to conquer for the Lord. Their prayers and the proclamation of the Word of God will be heard afar off, and lost souls will be drawn into the Kingdom of God.

A new set of believers will arise in our time—a troop of soldiers whose intention is to intercede for others. These fervent praying individuals and groups will go beyond their personal needs, gains, and blessings, and the Lord will baptise them with the oil of prayer

The Spirit of grace and supplication will drive them to their knees to seek the face of God. They will burn with passion in their closets, and in their corporate prayers they will ignite the dry, give drink to the thirsty, and spread their wings like eagles so that others may rise and fly upon them. Praying without ceasing will be the order of their lifestyle.

A GENERATION OF PRAYER

This generation will go deeper and taste of the harmony that is available in the depth of the Spirit. The sweet fellowship of the Holy Spirit will be their daily portion and experience, in their closet.

When such men step into their daily activities in society, it will be evident from their interactions that they are different. A sweet aroma will surround them, sensed by all who encounter these people of God. Ultimately, Jesus will be revealed through their conversations, actions, and reactions.

Prayer will no more be taught as a topic only, but it will be practiced as a heavenly culture, once we interiorise it. We will become men and women of prayer. A generation of prayer. We will receive divine wisdom to go about our daily affairs through prayer, and have access to knowledge, to advance in life, through prayer.

Our pulpits and pews will be filled with prayer and the hearts of men in the corridors of our churches will burn with prayer. Prayers will be stored in our hearts until our lips utter them out.

WE SHALL MARCH IN OUR RANKS

The Lord will release prisoners as we mount up prayers from our secret places and temples. Chains and shackles will be broken as we lift up our voice as one army ready for battle. Principalities, powers and territorial spirits will lose their control over the atmosphere as the Church of God roars in the Spirit. Our generation will truly experience a true advancement of the Kingdom of God.

Non will be limited among us. As we put on the whole armour of God, we shall line up as legions for the Kingdom of God. Men assigned to damage the kingdom of darkness and reclaim every inch of territory taken by Satan and his demons.

We shall march in our ranks and the Lord of Host will be our Captain. As we surrender to His total will and obey His full counsel with our whole hearts, He will strengthen us like never before. He will shine His face upon us. Our altars will never lack fire and oil will always be poured to keep the light shining.

We shall receive inner strength and the Lord will sharpen our sensitivity to be ever conscious of His ways and modus operandi. The presence of God will be our daily quest and as we walk on our streets and corridors of our temple, demons will recognise the sons of God and flee at our command in the name of Jesus.

This is the reality of the new generation that will make the Lord their ultimate goal and deliver themselves on the altar of sacrifice, as instruments of the Lord. Men who will be totally devoted to the life of prayer.

STRONGER THAN ANY FORCE OF DARKNESS

A generation whose heart has been restrained and confined by the love of God to seek the good of His Kingdom, the salvation of souls in their neighbour and their coming into the knowledge and the fullness of Christ, their Lord. Such men are the tools of these last days.

They are instruments made ready for the advancement of the Kingdom of God on earth. They are stronger than any force of darkness, they shine brighter in deep darkness and their voices echo in the chambers of evil—detaining God's people.

These are men secretly made by the Lord. They are God's people and independent of their occupation, job, career and social class, they are fully yielded to the Holy Spirit, they are called the sons of God, and they live a life dedicated and devoted to prayer.

The purpose and meaning of our lives must be shaped by the continuous interactions with our Lord in prayer. He yearns to commune daily with us in prayer and this is what we were created for. Simply to remain in Him forever. Our only true heart desire!

These are some few selected Bible verses on prayer and devotion:

Luke 6:12; Mark 1:35; 1 Thessalonians 5:16-18; Hebrews 4:16; Philippians 4:6-7; 1 John 5:14-15; Mark 11:24; Ephesians 6:17-18; 1 Timothy 2:1; James 5:16; Colossians 4:2; Jeremiah 29:12; Acts 13:1-4; Jeremiah 33:3; Acts 1:14; Acts 16:25; 1 Peter 4:7; James 1:6; Matthew 6:6; Psalm 18:6; Psalm 145:18.

CHAPTER 15

Discipleship & Discipline

According to the Cambridge online dictionary, *a disciple is simply a person who believes in the ideas and principles of someone and tries to live the way that person does or did.*

Truly, in biblical terms, as portrayed by the examples of Jesus, a disciple does not only spend time intellectually learning the practices of his Master, but furthermore, a disciple is possessed by the same Spirit behind the principles being taught, and, above all, he or she has the lifetime mandate to replicate the same teachings and to raise others just as they have been raised.

That is to say, discipleship is imitating the teacher's life, inculcating his values, and reproducing his teachings to others. In simple words, a true disciple can be recognised both in the words and deeds of his or her Master.

In the Christian context, Jesus and His disciples are the uttermost examples of discipleship. These were mere men called to be with the Lord, *(to learn, receive and interiorise the life and teachings of Jesus).* It incorporated their whole lives.

A disciple—according to this order—is known to others by the nature of his or her Master. Peter the fisherman was recognised by a young girl because of the way he looked. The early believers were called Christians because people saw the lifestyle of their Master in and on them. In other words, they portrayed whom they followed.

EVERYTHING ABOUT THEM REFLECTED JESUS

They did what their Master did and had taught them to do. They were not only filled in their heads with information and knowledge, but everything about them reflected Jesus, who had departed to heaven, but was evidently now residing in their hearts by His Spirit.

According to Barna Research, while the majority of Christians experience some form of relational investment in spiritual growth, sadly just 28% of Christians are actively involved in discipleship/community—a category that includes both those being discipled and those discipling others *(Barna Group, 2022).*

The study shows that a Christian in a discipleship programme is likely to be more energised from time to time, producing a more constant and faithful relationship with God, as well as more committed behaviour towards their faith, their local and universal Church of God.

If there is a serious case that needs to be addressed, then discipleship is the first on the list. In my short life and with the little experience I have had, I can barely count the number of believers who are really interested in sitting at the feet of a pastor or church leader to be taught and trained.

SPIRITUAL MATURITY IS PRECEDED BY SPIRITUAL HUNGER

With the absence of a gradual ABC discipleship training programme in the Church, it will be hard to raise a set of people who will be totally committed to the things of God. Bible study programmes and prayers, including reaching others, are a must for the well-being of any living church.

I have witnessed numerous debates and arguments among believers from all ranges of years on matters which were clearly basic and elementary, if only they had opened their Bibles on their shelves, or if they had allowed themselves to be properly taught by someone who knew better, for example, a teacher in a local ministry.

The difficulty of some preachers in going into the deep things of God while ministering is because they might, and will surely, miss more than half of the hearers. Some are evidently dull in understanding, not necessarily because of their educational background, but rather due to a lack of hunger for God and depth in the Scriptures.

Many are born again alright, but were never told to take the next step necessary, like growing spiritually in their faith, in order to bear fruit. This is the malady of our days: a class of well-intended believers who have not been properly taught the elementary principles, as well as moving on gradually to partake of stronger meat like the Word of righteousness, the anointing, the basis of deliverance, stewardship, and the accountability of every believer.

A TRUE BELIEVER'S LIFE IS AN EVER INCREASING LIGHT

This has created a loophole in the Body of Christ, and the issue needs to be confronted in this generation, as God grants us the grace. Any church in a given locality, which has no plan for the new convert and younger ones in their growth, will reap a set of unbalanced, unstable and improperly nurtured believers.

Who—despite their sincerity and love for God—may not be able to rightly divide the Word of God, and can therefore be easily moved to and fro by their emotions, external circumstances and any doctrine presented to them by someone which may be unscriptural.

Superstitious beliefs and fables have substituted the spiritual things in some Christian circles due to improper discipleship. Some have no knowledge of spiritual things and as a result of this the outcome of their life is a superficial lifestyle sustained by ideas and their culture. A true believer's life is a shining light which is ever increasing.

CHAPTER 16

Those who Neglect Discipleship Are Easy Prey for Darkness

Failure to progressively grow in the Christian faith is like a tree that bears no fruit. Such a tree is a waste in the farm, it only occupies space and hinders the fruit bearing ones. This generation is desperately in need of teachers; spiritual fathers who will properly train us in the ways of God.

It is humbling yet fruitful for a young believer to submit himself to the teaching ministry of his pastor or anyone he knows can help him grow. It is my deepest joy to be part of Followers of Christ International Ministry, Novara, Italy, where I have had the opportunity to be continuously discipled by Apostle Benjamin Ayim Asare, my Father in the Lord.

It is an undeniable fact that he who is discipled cannot remain ignorant forever. I am still miles behind where I desire to be, but the journey with the Lord under his mentorship has helped me recognise what the Lord has for me. The Bible is and remains a closed book and dead letter to the spiritually unlearned and untrained.

And as Timothy will carefully follow Paul so I desire to do so faithfully with my tutor and mentor. He has fed me to become hungrier and thirstier for God and His Kingdom. I am ever grateful. May God bless him.

SECULAR-CONSCIOUSNESS VS. JESUS-CONSCIOUSNESS

It is frightening to know how the Bible has been neglected as the bread for our spirit. The only words of life said Peter. We have more University degree holders and academicians than any other generation. People who have read complicated, voluminous and complex manuals as I have also, in order to pass an hour or two exams for certificates that will eventually perish.

Very few have dived into the simplicity of the Word of God, yet we brag of our knowledge and know-how. What a pity if this generation doesn't humble itself—to burn the candle—to retain the knowledge of God, encapsulated in the writings of the Holy Scriptures.

A learned man like Paul will make a staggering statement like, *"counting everything as loss,"* worthless for the excellency of the knowledge of Christ Jesus our Lord. We will likewise do the same if we want Jesus to be seen in us. Whoever neglects the art of being discipled or fathered by a human shepherd is an easy prey for darkness.

> Yet all of the accomplishments that I once took credit for, I've now forsaken them and I regard it all as nothing compared to the delight of experiencing Jesus Christ as my Lord! To truly know him meant letting go of everything from my past and throwing all my boasting on the garbage heap. It's all like a pile of manure to me now, so that I may be enriched in the reality of knowing Jesus Christ and embrace him as Lord in all of his greatness.
>
> Philippians 3:7-8 TPT

It is absurd to see how the youth of our time are more secular-conscious than Jesus-conscious, because we have fully neglected His words for the knowledge of this world, which is foolishness compared to the wisdom of God.

CHURCHES ARE RESPONSIBLE TO DISCIPLE THEIR YOUTH

Young committed Christians are called bigots for believing in an eternal deity. The Master Creator of the universe is exchanged for chaos, while His moral values and principles are no more suitable for our current society and lifestyle. The shame of this idiocy has led many young Christians to doubt their faith and even abandon what they once held to be true.

All because very few churches take the responsibility to disciple their youth. As they step outside the church auditorium, they have no place in their schedule to structurally learn their Bible.

Our days of the week are over-scheduled, and there is no place for an hour or two for a Bible class or prayer meeting. Indeed, the cost is high, but the price to pay in the future is unbearable.

Local churches must arise and leaders in the Body of Christ should reconsider and have a deep thought on how the churches will look. Philosophy and human wisdom will one day replace the infallible Word of God. Human knowledge will replace godly revelation and stony hearts will substitute hearts of flesh.

TO EMBRACE THE FOOLISHNESS OF THE CROSS

Entertainment will take the place of worship and another spirit will lead the service, consequently self-motivating messages—will be the gospel we preach. Strategic planning will replace prayer, while the promptings, convictions and leadings of the Spirit of the Lord will be an—old school doctrine—to this highly educated generation.

I hope for a remnant of young believers who will be knowledgeable in the Word of God. Youth highly discipled in the affairs of God. Young people who will rightly divide and defend the Bible as the only abiding and living Word of God capable of revealing the whole state of man from his origin to his future.

Young men and women who will share the whole counsel of God without shame and will joyfully embrace the *foolish message of the cross* in the face of a perverted and sinful world system—seeking to erase God from every affair of human life.

A GENERATION BOLDLY BIRTHED ON IT'S KNEES

A generation boldly birthed on its knees and brought up in the ways of the Lord, people who will recognise and acknowledge the endeavours of their fathers and carry the banner of their faith across borders. Churches in these days will be once again called Zion—where deliverers and saviours are forged—to continue the work of the Lord.

I pray for a generation that will faithfully serve their pastors and leaders like Joshua, Elisha, Eleazar of Damascus, the mighty men of David, Timothy, and Titus—people with teachable and humble spirits, ready to learn from those who know better than they do.

The short story of Apollos in the Bible is one that strikes me each time I come across it in Acts chapter 18. He wasn't ignorant of the counsel of God, but he had a loophole. Thank God he submitted to the ministry of Priscilla and Aquila. A couple gifted by God in teaching.

How arrogant our generation is. How difficult it is for us to acknowledge and confess that which we do not know. Instead, we pretend and ignore it or bluff around it. What a shame. Indeed, we look smart from the outside, but we are the most deceived.

The fear of the Lord has almost vanished from the hearts of men and from churches today. Distraction is the order of the day. Untrained believers are not disciplined enough to remain in the presence of God. Certain people keep up a stream of distracting conversation during the service, and these interruptions cut off the flow of the Spirit while the speaker is ministering.

ELISHA: BOTH DISCIPLE & SERVANT RECEIVED A DOUBLE PORTION

Indeed, our spiritual sensitivity is at its lowest level. The telephone has taken seat in the hearts of men—as their primary god—and some cannot do without this device, both in their homes and churches, as it rings continuously during meetings. It is a thorn in the flesh in our day. During a meeting I attended, more than three phones rang during the service, and the preacher was deeply grieved—so was I. The Holy Spirit in me couldn't bear such an act.

Men are not disciplined enough to respect God nor their neighbour sat beside them. Will the churches notice this abhorrent act in the presence of God and limit its usage? My generation is in this valley and only by strict discipleship and discipline can we silence this idol in our midst.

Elisha chose to follow a hard and unpredictable man like Elijah. He served him faithfully, even washing his hands as described—being not only a disciple but also a servant to him. No wonder he could ask for, and ultimately receive, a double portion of his anointing.

The idea of following another human being with the intention of learning from them sounds very strange to the believer in the twenty-first century—let alone serving them. *"After all, we are all children of God and anointed by Him,"* is the reply of the rebellious and unruly Christian.

We quote portions of Scripture to defend our deceived, unrenewed minds. We embrace those interpretations that relieve us from any sacrifice or cross to bear—sacrifices that are eternally relevant. We prefer the blessings of God over knowing our responsibilities towards Him, His Church, and His creation.

THEIR PURSUIT OF GOD IS NOT SELF-SERVING

Our pursuit for God is primarily based on requests and faith to receive—but less open hearts and strengthened shoulders—to share in the burdens, yokes and weights of the Lord. A properly discipled believer acknowledges the totality of the Kingdom of God, he knows everything is surrendered and measured by the rod of the Word.

Jesus is the Master, the beginning and the end glory of all the affairs of the Christian life. This believer is blessed because of the Kingdom of God, and his ultimate goal is to become a blessing to others. He is strengthened to strengthen others, empowered to empower others, enlightened to do so to others, comforted to comfort others. He is taught to teach others.

For such believers, the greatest desire of their hearts is that God be blessed, receive all the glory and honour, and that His Kingdom advances. This is the very heartbeat and purpose of their lives. Our generation will make no progress unless we break this trend and position ourselves to be properly trained, discipled, and lovingly disciplined.

THEY HAVE A KINGDOM-FIRST MENTALITY

This is the moment when pride, arrogance and selfish gain is eradicated and Kingdom purposes become the number one goal. Errors will die by themselves and deception will find no fertile ground in our midst. People will be highly sensitive to the Holy Spirit and they will witness within themselves – the truth when spoken.

These are few selected Bible verses on discipleship and discipline:

2 Timothy 2:1-2; Philippians 2:19-24; Luke 9:23-24; John 15:16-17; Colossians 1:28-29; Matthew 28:18-20; John 8:31; 1 Peter 2:21; 1 Corinthians 11:1/3:5-9; Titus 1:4; Galatians 4:19

Final Thoughts

To the remnant of this generation—those whose hearts pant after God and who desperately desire to walk with Him—my humble word is this: the eternal life we receive from Him is more powerful than any human ideology or religious spirit. Our purpose in life is to make room for the influence of the Kingdom of God, both in our time and when we go to glory.

TRANSFORMED INTO HIS IMAGE

From this little exhortation, I desire to draw my generation to the consciousness of living for the Kingdom of God and its advancement, rather than settling for a cold, firm, traditional, and ritualistic Christian lifestyle. Such a lifestyle produces no life but keeps men in chains and bondage.

Whoever holds this whole-souled manuscript yet has no idea of the true reality of a New Testament believer, should call on the name of Jesus. For in that name alone has God deposited the saving power for every soul.

Then simply get a Bible for your personal reading—study and meditate—in order to become acquainted with this eternal loving Person. Pay close attention to every word in that Book of books, for in it and through prayer we are transformed into His image.

ACCORDING TO THE STANDARD OF HIS WORD

Ask the Holy Spirit in prayer to reveal Himself and teach you how to walk in the newness of life empowered by the resurrected Christ. Then finding a spiritually healthy church is the next key, where one can grow and have godly fellowship with other sons and daughters of God.

The Church is the bride of Jesus, and she lives by every jot of His Word, inspired by the Holy Spirit. The born-again believer today cannot afford to live below the standard of the truth of Scripture, neither can he allow himself to be led astray by falsehood, man-made traditions, or cultures.

Our society—including some churches—commune at the table of Jezebel and have drunk from the cup of spiritual adultery. Such subtle yet evil deeds have degraded the influence of the Church in our society.

A dreadful end awaits the bride who doesn't purge and separate herself from such acts, because the Bridegroom comes for a pure and undefiled bride—who has washed her garments in His blood—and is filled with and led by the Holy Spirit in all her doings. His eyes are like flames of fire and every work will be tested by them.

Culture and the traditions of men have always made an attempt—in every generation—to put the reality of our God in a shadow, and has highlighted the activities and initiatives of men without, the promptings of the Holy Spirit.

These are weak and temporal duties without any true spiritual value. They are too weak—in every aspect—to draw the hearts of men to God. It all sums up to mere religious practices and men have embraced this phenomenon throughout the generations.

BORN TO PORTRAY THE EXCELLENCY OF HIS NATURE

No human culture or tradition can fully portray the excellency of the nature of God. The pure knowledge of the divine has been faintly and superficially sought— generation after generation—have suffered this malady, causing men to walk in darkness and in the swamp of sin.

I sincerely urge the youth of today—who are looking for God—to widely and unreservedly open their hearts and approach these writings without misconceptions or prejudice. With the solemn guide of the Bible and prayer—read and re-read—while speaking to Jesus in your heart, because He is nearer to us than we can imagine.

As you read, proceed faithfully in your pursuit of God. He will knock at the door of your heart, and these inner promptings *(though silent)* will yet be loudly heard and perceived by every fibre of your being. Let Him in as you acknowledge and confess Him as your Saviour and Lord—

who was crucified and resurrected for your personal sins—that you may live in and for Him.

You will be amazed with the precision dealings and effectiveness of the Holy Spirit within your human spirit. Blessed moments of intimacy will cause you to want to know Him more and more.

God has put eternity in the heart of every man as the preacher says in the book of Ecclesiastes. This God-given awareness will never let man be free from seeking Him. Paraphrased by Saint Augustine in his famous quote, *"You have made us for Yourself, oh Lord, and our hearts are restless until they rest in you."*

These statements point to something deeper and richer than mere cultural or traditional knowledge can give any man. Only in the pursuit and desperate hunger for Jesus can any person know God.

No matter how far you are from God or your perception of Him may be, I dearly submit to you that He is the very thing you have been in search of your whole life. His will is to reveal Himself to you, if you will seek Him diligently with all of your heart, just as He has promised in the Scriptures.

His desire is to dwell inside His masterpiece—His prize creation—man. You are therefore of more value to Him than all of creation put together. He profoundly loves you. Don't live or die without Him. You simply can't afford to pay that kind of price!

To the Sincere Lover of God

If it has indeed dawned in your heart to be part of this empty—yet desperate—generation who seek to know God as He wants to be known, you are not alone. Consider the examples of the holy men and women in the Bible—they sought and found God for their generation. We will not relent or give up until we do so for ours.

Keep us daily on our knees
As we behold your face
We are hungry for you God.

Endnotes

- Ayim Asare, Benjamin. Life Is a Priceless Treasure: Living Now to Live Tomorrow. 2008.
- Ayim Asare, Benjamin. The Pursuit of Power Versus Fruits. Muelheim, Germany: Freshmanna Publication, House of Solution, 2019.
- Bounds, E. M. Power Through Prayer. (Public domain; originally published 1912.)
- Barna Group. Two in Five Christians Are Not Engaged in Discipleship [Blog post]. Published 26 January 2022. Available at: https://www.barna.com/research/christians-discipleship-community/ (Accessed: [2025]).
- Cambridge University Press. *Cambridge English Dictionary.* Retrieved from https://dictionary.cambridge.org (2025)
- Pateman, Alan. Truth for the Journey: Letters to the Church. Italy: APMI Publications Italy, 2023. Chapters 7, 28, 32–34.
- Prince, Derek. Authority and Power of God's Word. Whitaker House, 2009.
- Ravenhill, Leonard. Why Revival Tarries. Minneapolis, MN: Bethany House, 2004. ISBN 0-7642-2905-2 (pbk).
- Saint Augustine, *Confessions,* trans. Henry Chadwick (Oxford: Oxford University Press, 1991), Book I, Chapter 1: *Fecisti nos ad te*

et inquietum est cor nostrum… generally translated as "You made us for Yourself, O Lord, and our hearts are restless until they rest in You."

- Smelser, N. J., & Baltes, P. B. (Eds.). (2001). International encyclopaedia of the social & behavioural sciences. Amsterdam: Elsevier.
- White, Leslie A. "Philosophy & Religion. History and Society, Culturology. Cultural Evolution." *Encyclopaedia Britannica.* Written and fact-checked by the Editors of Encyclopaedia Britannica. Retrieved from https://www.britannica.com.
- Scripture taken from the New King James Version®. Copyright © 1982 by Thomas Nelson. Used by permission. All rights reserved.
- Scripture references marked AMP are taken from the Amplified® Bible, Copyright © 2015 by The Lockman Foundation. Used by permission.
- Scripture quotations marked TPT are from The Passion Translation®. Copyright © 2017, 2018, 2020 by Passion & Fire Ministries, Inc. Used by permission. All rights reserved. ThePassionTranslation.com

Ministry Profile

Emmanuel Sarfo Acheampong is a passionate disciple of Christ. Throughout the years, he has devoted himself to the study of God's Word and other Christian literature and teaching materials, in order to be an efficient teacher both in and outside the Church. He has dedicated himself to understanding the Scriptures, and has served faithfully as a Sunday School Bible teacher at the Followers of Christ International Church, Novara, Italy, while also sitting under Apostle Dr. Benjamin Ayim Asare's weekly Bible Course, *School of Ministry for Potential Leaders (SOMFPL)*, for many years.

The author is deeply committed to the unity, love, and spiritual awakening of young adults in the body of Christ. He has set his heart to pursue the Lord and to know His Word. This pursuit has made him skilled in teaching and preaching with authority, because he has prepared his heart to live out what he teaches – not merely accumulating knowledge, but immersing himself in the text. Therefore, his teaching is not a separate activity, but a natural consequence of his devotion and understanding.

His heartbeat is to see the Kingdom of God expand and transform the hearts of people, churches, and society. Above all, he longs to see Christ fully formed in all believers—especially the youth—as we surrender totally to the Lord and are properly discipled by His servants, so that we may be ready and prepared for the greater harvest.

Emmanuel earned his bachelor's degree in Political Science and International Relations from the University of Eastern Piedmont "Amedeo Avogadro" *(UPO),* Alessandria. He resides in Novara, Italy, with his family.

To Contact the Author

Please email:

Emmanuel Sarfo Acheampong
Email: emmanuelsarfoacheampong@yahoo.it

Please include your prayer requests and comments when you write.

APMI Publishing and Publications is committed to providing you with an affordable and easy way to publish your books making them available as paperback, hardcover, and/or eBook copies on international outlets.
Contact us today!

www.alanpatemanworldmissions.com/publications
Tel. 0039 366 329 1315; publications@alanpatemanworldmissions.com

www.ingramcontent.com/pod-product-compliance
Lightning Source LLC
Chambersburg PA
CBHW060008050426
42448CB00028B/1716